S0-BXZ-506

Geography Matters®

Trail Guide
to
U.S. Geography

By Cindy Wiggers

Acknowledgments

Special thanks to my dear husband, Josh, for all of his input, assistance, and technical expertise and for providing all the maps - always putting my projects ahead of his own.

Thanks to my sister, Kim Weber (whitmoreweber.com), for graciously sharing her photography skills on a moment's notice.

To Debbie Strayer, thank you for your prayers and valuable input. Your insight on developing learning skills helped make the revised edition even more user-friendly.

Copyright 2003 Cindy Wiggers
Second edition Copyright 2005 Cindy Wiggers
Revised edition Copyright 2007 Cindy Wiggers

Published by Geography Matters, Inc.

Edited by Janet Farmer and Jane Willis
Second edition edited by Mary Jo Tate

Book layout by Libby Wiggers
Photography by Kim Whitmore-Weber

All rights reserved. No part of this book may be reproduced in any form without permission from the publisher except by a reviewer who wishes to quote brief passages in review. Permission is granted to photocopy appendix pages meant for Student Notebook for the use of one family or one classroom only. Purchase of this book does not entitle reproduction of any part of this book for an entire school, district, or system. Such use is strictly prohibited.

ISBN: 978-1-931397-19-3

Library of Congress Control Number: 2002113561

Printed in the United States of America

Geography Matters, Inc.
800.426.4650
www.geomatters.com

Geography Matters®
Trail Guide to U.S. Geography
By Cindy Wiggers

Table of Contents

Geography Matters®
Trail Guide to U.S. Geography

Greetings fellow Geography buffs and all,

This book is one of a series of three geography Trail Guides, all written with the busy teacher in mind.

Each Trail Guide is flexible, provides progressive skill development for students of all ages, and makes learning geography fun and memorable. With a little guidance the first two or three weeks most students will work independently the remainder of the year.

The Trail Guide is designed to encourage a student notebooking approach to learning. By the end of the year students will have compiled a thorough, colorful record of their geography journey that they will be proud to keep and show their own children in years to come.

Define Your Objectives

There are a variety of ways to use this three-part manual. Determine your goals for teaching geography, and place students on the trail that meets your objectives. These three sections are explained in the following pages.

- GEOGRAPHY TRAILS - five-minute drills
- POINTS OF INTEREST - mapping, research, and projects
- GEOGRAPHY THROUGH LITERATURE - Lewis and Clark Expedition

Take a hike on the GEOGRAPHY TRAILS by following one of three trail markers and having students answer questions using a U.S. atlas or almanac. You'll find the answer key for all three trails starting on page 133. Step off the trail for POINTS OF INTEREST where students make their own maps and blaze a trail with a wide assortment of hands-on activities and research projects. For added interest students can call or write state tourism departments for maps, brochures, and state information. Tourism department addresses and toll-free numbers can be found in any almanac.

Wrap up the year on an adventure with the Lewis and Clark Expedition by reading *The Captain's Dog, My Journey with the Lewis and Clark Tribe*. This unit study provides mapping, vocabulary, and additional activity choices combining literature with U.S. geography. You might consider using the Lewis and Clark unit as interesting summer reading project.

If you wish to simply introduce some geography this year, or to lay a foundation for a future in-depth study of U.S. geography, or if your objective is to reinforce and review the topic, the five-minute drills will meet your goal. You may opt to just assign mapping this year. Or if you purchased this course to teach a thorough U.S. geography course or to inspire students to learn about the states, geographical features, and more, plan to incorporate all three parts into your lesson plans.

However you use the U.S. Trail Guide, from the GEOGRAPHY TRAILS daily drills to the POINTS OF INTEREST and the literature unit, your students are sure to enjoy a memorable geography experience.

Bon Voyage!
Cindy Wiggers

[Additional Note: Since I covered in detail how to teach geography in *The Ultimate Geography and Timeline Guide*, I have not done so again here. If you need more direction regarding the subject of geography, if you want more mapping assignments, or if you plan to incorporate your U.S. history studies with geography get a copy of this book. Besides being a basic teacher refresher course, it includes a ton of reproducibles, literature, science, and history units, and a whole section on using timelines.]

Using the Trail Guide to U.S. Geography

Regions

This course addresses state studies by dividing them into seven geographical regions. According to Webster's dictionary a region is a "large and indefinite part of the surface of the earth." Therefore, the U.S. can be divided in a variety of ways. For the purpose of this study the following regions and the states comprising those regions are:

New England	Maine	New Hampshire	Connecticut
	Massachusetts	Vermont	Rhode Island
Mid-Atlantic	New York	Pennsylvania	Maryland
	New Jersey	West Virginia	Delaware
South	North Carolina	Kentucky	South Carolina
	Virginia	Tennessee	Georgia
	Alabama	Arkansas	Florida
	Mississippi	Louisiana	
Midwest	Ohio	Indiana	Wisconsin
	Michigan	Illinois	Minnesota
	Iowa	North Dakota	Nebraska
	Missouri	South Dakota	Kansas
Southwest	Oklahoma	New Mexico	
	Texas	Arizona	
Rocky Mountain	Montana	Wyoming	Utah
	Idaho	Colorado	Nevada
Pacific Coast	Washington	California	Alaska
	Oregon		Hawaii

Instructions
Making a State Notebook

This curriculum manual is based upon a student notebook method of study. Each week students add to their State Notebook, developing a priceless record of their U.S. geography study for the year. A few important helpful hints to share with students to establish this notebook follow:

- Use your best penmanship.
- Add to the notebook each week.
- Include drawings, reports, pictures, maps, charts, and reproducible sheets from the appendix.
- Keep the notebook in a safe place where it will not be misplaced or damaged.
- Show your notebook to others, look at the notebooks of your friends, and tell them how nice their notebooks are. Look at other books for inspiration. Let your notebook provide others with good ideas.
- Be creative. Your notebook will reflect your interests and abilities.

Trail Guide to U.S. Geography Student Notebook Files

Your students can create their own state notebook from instructions that follow or you may wish to use the supplementary *Trail Guide to U.S. Geography Student Notebook*. The Student Notebook is available online as a downloadable eBook or on a CD-ROM. These PDF files are printable notebook pages that form the framework for the State Notebook and include:

- Geography Trails questions with a space to place the answer
- Mapping assignment lists
- Outline maps needed for each week
- Customized templates for completing two Trail Blazing projects each week
- Generic templates for completing nearly any Trail Blazing projects

Select Geography Trails and Trail Blazing assignments. Print the pages from your computer, three hole punch, and place in a 3-ring binder. You can choose Student Notebook files for each level or purchase all three levels in one disk (or eBook). If you decide to provide the Student Notebook, it includes all the outline maps. You will not need to purchase additional outline maps as listed with the additional resources.

Please understand the Student Notebook CD-ROM (or eBook) is not a required resource. It is designed to help simplify creating the State Notebook. Most students can create their own State Notebook with the instructions that follow.

Notebook Instructions

Organize a three-ring binder with the following eight sections:

> New England
> Mid-Atlantic
> South
> Midwest
> Southwest
> Rocky Mountain
> Pacific Coast
> Geography Terms

You may decide to add other sections, such as one for Lewis and Clark, later.

Regional Divisions

Place two maps in the front of each region section of the State Notebook. One is an outline map of the U.S. with the region shaded; this map shows the region in context. The second is an outline map of the region itself. Place completed mapping assignments, reports, and projects in the correct region of the notebook behind these two maps.

1. Make one copy of each outline map of the seven regions from *Uncle Josh's Outline Map Book* or CD-ROM. Shade the region map with the physical features, using a physical map of the United States as a reference. Label each state.
2. Make seven copies of the U.S. outline map, one for each of the seven regions. Label each map in the margin with the name of a region. Shade the appropriate states that make up the region.

There are four core projects for the State Notebook:

- States of the Union
- State Your Questions
- Signature State
- Face the Facts (completed for the region)

You can use the same project for each state or mix them up for variety. If your students include at least one of these three assignments for each state or the "Face the Facts" project for each region, in their notebooks they will have the foundational data for all fifty states by the end of the year. Select any other projects according to interest, abilities, and time available, and place them in the notebook in the appropriate region section.

These are guidelines for organizing the notebook. Be flexible and feel free to use your own ideas. There's probably no wrong way to put it together. You may decide to include more or less material. If you let the students design their own notebooks with your guidance, they will take ownership of them and may even do a better job than you ever expected. Let the notebooks serve to reflect each student's character and personality.

Geography Trails Instructions

Take your students on a hike down the GEOGRAPHY TRAILS section of this book, where they complete daily geography drills in about five minutes a day. Using an atlas or almanac, you will provide them an opportunity to develop and improve research skills, think logically, and build a geography foundation through daily geoMoments.

Following one of the three GEOGRAPHY TRAILS markers, students answer two questions per day, four days a week. The flexibility of the Trail Guide series allows you to take one student through the book for three years or three levels of students all at the same time in one year. These three trails are marked according to skill development and topics, not necessarily by age or grade. Take primary students down the first trail. Some primary level students may not be ready to answer questions alone, so plan to do them together. Show them how to find the answers in their atlas. Perhaps use only one question per day with the younger students.

Additional recommendation: If students make a chart of facts the first week of each new region using the topics below, they can use it as a reference for answering some of the GEOGRAPHY TRAILS questions. (See "Face the Facts" instructions starting on page 13.)

Questions on the Primary trail cover the following topics:

capitals	boundaries
location	rivers, oceans, gulfs, bays
mountains	postal abbreviations
landforms	state nicknames
state birds	state trees
cardinal directions (north, east, south, and west)	

Please note: levels are based more on thinking ability rather than age. Grade levels are approximate:
Primary: grades 3-5
Intermediate: grades 5-8
Secondary: grades 8-high school

 Questions on the Intermediate trail address some of the topics above plus:

area	time zones (time zone map provided in appendix)
places	lakes and other places with water
national parks	longitude/latitude (30°N 84°W)
cities	intermediate directions (NE, NW, SE, and SW)

 Students who follow the Secondary trail will develop research skills by using an almanac to locate facts and statistics about the states. Students assess whether to use an atlas or almanac to correctly answer their questions. The questions become progressively more difficult as students become more familiar with using the almanac. Some topics include:

agriculture	industry	longitude/latitude (44°N 68°W)
population	landforms	climate and weather
economy	bridges	state comparisons

Although *The World Almanac and Book of Facts*, published annually by World Almanac Books since 1886, was used to generate questions for this trail, students should be able to use any good current almanac. Students may also refer to their atlas to answer some questions.

Using an Almanac

Take a few minutes to help your students become familiar with the index and table of contents of the almanac. You will notice, the almanac provides data for both the world and the U.S. Using the index, look for the section that summarizes each U.S. state. *The World Almanac and Book of Facts* is tabbed to make finding the different sections in the almanac easier. The first few weeks the answers to the GEOGRAPHY TRAILS can be found simply by using the "States" or "States of the Union" section of the almanac. As weeks go on students will use other parts of the almanac or combine data to form correct answers.

Calculating Answers from Data Provided

It is one thing to find answers to questions, but entirely different thinking skills are used to analyze different forms of data and draw conclusions. Therefore, starting in Week 4 students will begin to use more than one piece of data on the "States" section to calculate answers or to draw conclusions. This type of question helps students think on their own, not just find answers from the text.

Here's a sample question:
> **What percent of the land in New York is forested?**

The problem:
If the almanac does not provide this information by percentage, how do you answer the question?

The solution:
Calculate from data that you can locate in the almanac. If you know how many acres are forested and how much total area of land New York has, you can use those two numbers to answer the question.

The formula:

$$\% \text{ of forested land} = \frac{\text{forested land area}}{\text{total land area}} \times 100$$

Note: You must use the same unit of measure for forested land as is used for total land. If the almanac provides one in acres and one in square miles, convert the acres to square miles. There are 640 acres in every square mile of land. To convert acres to square miles divide by 640.

$$\text{square miles} = \frac{\text{acres}}{640}$$

Formulas are provided on the Student Reference Sheet on page 121 and again in the answer key for your convenience.

Why all this calculation in a geography book?
So much of schoolwork is reading text and answering questions (often in the same order as the text), requiring little real thinking. Many of the almanac questions are designed to help students get out of the rut of read-and-answer and to thinking with their very own brain cells how to assess data available in order to answer correctly.

Consider how discovery learning may take place with the sample question above. Because students have had more exposure to New York City than the state of New York, some students may not recognize that the entire state is NOT like the city. Perhaps most students envision the state as being full of buildings, concrete, taxis, and LOTS of people. By calculating the answer to this question, students will discover that over half of the state of New York is forested. This discovery learning is where true education is taking place!

Further Progression
Starting in Week 8 students following the Secondary trail marker will take another step in finding answers to *GEOGRAPHY TRAILS* questions. Answers are no longer confined to the "States" section of the almanac, but are located in other sections where U.S. data is given. Instruct students to use the index and table of contents for key words from the questions. An example from Week 8 follows.

The questions:
> What are the high and low altitudes of North Carolina and where are they? How many miles of Atlantic Ocean coastline does Virginia have?

Finding answers:
If the "States" section does not provide altitude information, it will be located somewhere else in the almanac. Identify key words from the question and find them in the index. In the first question above, the key word is "altitude(s)." Find the key word, turn to the page indicated, and start your search for the answer. You may have to flip a few pages - but keep looking for those key words. The key word for the second question is "coastline." Again locate the key word and turn to the page indicated. From that page find the information using "Atlantic," "coast,", or "Virginia" as key words. After the first few weeks this type of question is used, students will make this transition fairly easily with a bit of direction and by using the key word hints provided in parentheses.

Almanac Answers

Most answers in the Trail Guide do not change over time, so no matter what year almanac you use the answer key should remain the same. However, some answers may change from year to year, as annual editions of the almanac are published with the most current statistics. A few questions of this type are included to give students the opportunity to compare information from state to state and to learn what kind of up-to-date data an almanac provides.

Keep in mind, the goal of this curriculum is not to memorize a ton of facts. The objective is to develop research and thinking skills and teach almanac usage. Learn to recognize the type of question that may have a different answer than it did the year this book was published, and acknowledge that your student could have a more current answer than the answer key.

Answer Key

The answer key for each trail starts on page 133. All efforts have been made to ensure accuracy. Please report any errors to the publisher, and corrections will be made upon the next printing.

Recommended *GEOGRAPHY TRAILS* resources:

Children's Illustrated Atlas of the United States

The World Almanac and Book of Facts or other almanac

Optional:

For questions using longitude and latitude references, use a student world atlas or classroom atlas.

This section, divided by **Mapping** and **Trail Blazing**, provides weekly hands-on assignments and opportunities for research and reporting. There are more projects than any one student could possibly complete during the week, so don't even think about making your students do them all! Be flexible. Select assignments that fit well with your students' interest and learning styles, or let them choose for themselves. POINTS OF INTEREST can be used in a variety of ways:

1. Cover the basics of two states each week.
2. Choose one of the two states to study each week.
3. Divide your students into two groups, each studying a different state. Share information ina weekly oral show-and-tell type of presentation.
4. Study one state a week in depth and stretch the U.S. geography course over two years.

Refer to the sample schedules on page 18 for basic weekly lesson plan guidelines.

Mapping

Mapping assignments are a list of items students will draw or label on outline maps. The reproducible maps in *Uncle Josh's Outline Map Book* or CD-ROM are perfect to use for these assignments. You may prefer to use the printable Student Notebook CD-ROM or eBook created to go with this course. If so you will not need additional maps as they are included in the printable files.

Students will use the same atlas to fill in their outline maps as they use to answer the GEOGRAPHY TRAILS questions. Mapping assignments are separated by levels, however some students may want to do more. If so, please let them! Instruct them to use a star or to underline state capitals. All students who have had little to no experience labeling outline maps will need help the first week or two. Make sure they can "see" the information on the atlas that goes on their outline map. Help them transfer the data and give praise and encouragement freely. For basic guidelines on using maps read Chapter 3 in *The Ultimate Geography and Timeline Guide* or use *Discovering Maps* published by Hammond Inc.

Recommended **Mapping** resources for all students:
- *Uncle Josh's Outline Map Book* or CD-ROM OR
- Trail Guide to U.S. Geography Student Notebook (in CD-ROM or eBook)
- *Children's Illustrated Atlas of the United States*
- Colored pencils

Trail Blazing

The assignments choices in this section span all levels. Select projects that meet the thinking skills of your students. Trail markings provided for a handful of Secondary level assignments are included to assist you to know they are too advanced for Primary level students.

Geography Terms

Nestled in the **Trail Blazing** section about once a week is a shaded box identifying two geography terms to define. Include these definitions in a geography terms section in the student notebook. Students who enjoy drawing may like creating an Illustrated Geography Dictionary. Use the Illustrated Geography Dictionary template in the appendix for this project.

An especially useful visual aid for recognizing geography terms is the Geographical Terms Chart. It's a color, illustrated picture of geographical terms with physical features labeled right on the illustration. In addition, over 150 terms are defined on the back side. [See page 143 to obtain this item.]

Trail Guide to U.S. Geography
Points of Interest Instructions
Projects

Projects make learning fascinating and memorable. Instructions for a variety of interesting regional and state assignments follow. These activities are listed on the Student Reference Sheet on page 121. Copy page 121 and place in the front of the State Notebook for handy reference. Remember, do not compel students to do ALL projects on ALL states.

Allowing students to choose their own projects helps foster a positive attitude about doing the work. Some of the tasks are better suited to the region, some are best completed for a state, and some are appropriate for either. The instructions that follow are written directly to the student.

Regional Projects

On the first week of each new region, select from the list of regional activities for that region. Place a U.S. map with the region shaded and an outline map of the region marked with its physical features as the first two pages of each section of your State Notebook.

Face the Facts

Make the chart of facts for each region as you study them. Copy the template from the appendix. Place the names of the states in the first column. In the top row place the kind of facts you want to record. Now start filling in the chart. Here is a sample of New England's area and population to help you see how to set it up:

New England	Area	Population	Population Density
Maine	30,865	1,243,700	40
New Hampshire	8969	1,179,100	131
Vermont	9249	590,400	64
Massachusetts	7838	6,133,500	782
Connecticut	4845	3,271,100	675
Rhode Island	1045	987,000	944

You will find these facts in the U.S. atlas, almanac, kid's almanac, or other resources. You can calculate the population density yourself by dividing the population by the area. This tells how many people, if they were spread out evenly throughout the state, fit into each square mile of land. Choose from a variety of other facts for your chart: capital, date of statehood, state bird, state tree, state motto, state flower, state nickname, average income, and more. If you make a "Face the Facts" charts for each region before you begin, you can use it as a reference to answer many of the GEOGRAPHY TRAILS questions. Some GEOGRAPHY TRAILS topics are:

🐾 capital, bird, tree, postal abbreviation   🐾 area, nickname, rank by area, highest point

Students skilled with using a spreadsheet on the computer may prefer to make your own chart. A computer-generated spreadsheet will allow you to sort the data to list the states in order by population or area or whatever column you select to sort. Older students can develop thinking skills by com-

Points of Interest Instructions

paring information on the charts. It is fascinating what conclusions can be drawn from studying the finished chart. What state has the highest population? Which has the most land area? Are the largest states also the most populated? You can also use this kind of chart to memorize state facts.

Salt Dough Map
Make a salt dough map of the region (or the state). Here is a simple recipe.

> 2 parts flour
> 1 part salt
> 1 part water
>
> Mix ingredients together. If crumbly, add a little more water.

This mixture makes salt dough that can be used to make three-dimensional maps. Use an outline map as your guide. Tape it on the bottom of a piece of cardboard or a cardboard pop can case. Pile the salt dough on the map, spreading it out to the edges of the land area shown on the map. The dough should be thicker for mountainous regions and lower at valleys and rivers. Use a toothpick or other such tool to make crevices or physical detail. Let dry overnight (or a couple of days – depending upon how thick the map is). Paint with tempera paints or use food dye on dough before forming into the 3-D map.

Climate
Write a paragraph describing the climate and seasons of the region. Shade an outline map of the region according to temperature or rainfall in the summer and in the winter, or use it to depict the weather forecast on any given day. Include it after your paragraph and place in the State Notebook. Use a general reference atlas or classroom atlas for climate information.

Crossword Puzzle
Make a crossword puzzle using a grid. Give clues by the region or the state for words that run across and down. Use places, people, and terms of importance to each state or region as answers. Be sure to number the first box of each word and match the number with the across or down clue. Shade all unused boxes. Copy the puzzle to share with others and place one in the notebook according to region. Keep an unused copy of the puzzle in the back of that region.

State Projects

States of the Union
Make copies of "States of the Union" sheet from the appendix. Complete these information sheets weekly for each state or for the states of your choice. Write the name of the state on the line provided and the two-letter post office abbreviation on the line below. Using the U.S. atlas, a state-by-state guide, almanac, encyclopedia, or web addresses from an almanac, find the state facts and record them in the appropriate place on the sheet. Space is provided for drawings, printouts, or stickers of the state bird, tree, and flower. Shade in the state on the U.S. map in the upper corner of the sheet.

You can use this sheet for every state and place them together in one report folder to make a "States of the Union" booklet or use it in your State Notebook filed according to region.

State Your Questions
Copy the "State Your Question" sheet associated with your trail marker found in the appendix. Answer the questions as you study each state. Shade in the state on the U.S. map in the upper corner of the sheet. Place in your State Notebook according to region.

Trail Guide to U.S. Geography
Points of Interest Instructions

Signature State
Make your own outline map of a state by tracing one from an outline map. Here's a twist on it, though - instead of drawing a line around the paper in the shape of the state, write the name of the state around the paper in the shape of the state. Options: write the name of the state • capital • nickname • separated by dots or stars or hearts or whatever may represent the state. Draw and shade the physical features. Add a city or two, a national park, or any other information that interests you.

Here is an example of Colorado:

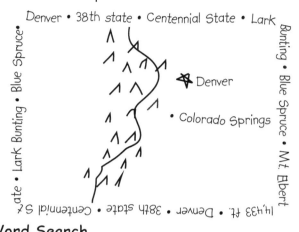

Option:
Fill in the map with a collage of pictures of state symbols, places, and landmarks. Get pictures from travel brochures, magazines, and books. Or copy pictures from books and color with colored pencils. Be creative. Place the images within the signature border of the state and secure with glue stick. Cover entire map with clear contact paper, three-hole-punch the page, and place in your State Notebook.

Word Search
Make your own word search using a grid. First make a list of the names of places, famous people, historical events, animals, plants, foods, or other topics related to the state or region you are studying. Write the letters in each cell of the grid, across, down, diagonally, and in reverse. Share letters from one word with another where they cross in the grid. Fill in the remaining boxes of the grid with other random letters. Make copies to share. Put a completed word search in your State Notebook according to region and keep an unused copy in the back of that region.

Go Team Go!
Use one of the reproducible forms in the appendix (according to your level). Learn about the places where your favorite sports teams play their home games. Using an almanac, Internet, encyclopedia, or library books, answer the questions on the sheet. Include a drawing or picture of the team logo. Place in your State Notebook.

Flags
Draw a picture of the state flag. Include information on what the colors and symbols mean.

Travel Brochure
Make a travel brochure advertising the beauty, landmarks, and historical sites of the state. Include drawings, pictures, descriptions, and more. Use an 8 1/2 x 11" sheet of paper folded into thirds. Or use an 8 1/2 x 14" sheet folded into fourths. Make copies to share with others. Find information from the state tourism department, Chambers of Commerce, Internet search, or any of your favorite resources.

Timeline
Using the timeline template in the appendix, make a history timeline of each state. Put dates along the line and write events in the spaces. For an interesting timeline include pictures and color.

Points of Interest Instructions

Eat Your Way Through the USA

Everyone loves to eat! Prepare and eat food typical of the state you are studying or with ingredients grown in the state. *Eat Your Way Through the USA,* a cookbook by Loreé Pettit, includes delicious recipes for a full meal from each state and additional fascinating food facts.

Economy and Industry

Write a paragraph or two about how the agriculture, climate, and natural resources are related to one other and how they affect the state's economy. Include an outline map of the state with symbols that show locations of agriculture, products, and industry.

Memorizing States and Capitals

Learn the states and capitals of the region during the 2-6 weeks you study each region, and continue to review them through the year. Some fun ways to do this are by making and using flashcards, playing Concentration (a memory game), and listening to geography songs.

Flashcards

Make a set of flashcards for each region. On one side of an index card draw an outline of the shape of the state. Place a dot or star on the location of the capital. On the back of the card write the name of the state and its capital. Show the card with drawing facing out. Players name the state or capital. Option: To aid in remembering other state symbols, list the state nickname, motto, flower, tree, and bird below the name of the state and capital. Play different rounds naming various topics.

Concentration

Make your own set of Concentration cards by cutting an index card in half. Place the name of a state on one card and the name of its capital on the other half. Shuffle the cards and place cards with words side down in rows on a table. The first player will turn up two cards. If the cards are a matching set of state and capital, he keeps the cards and goes again. If the cards do not match, turn the cards back down, and the next player takes a turn. When there are no cards left, the game is over. The player with the most cards wins. But really everyone wins if the game helps you learn the states and capitals!

Option: add state motto, bird, flower, nickname, etc. on the card with the state name (or use stickers or drawings). When you play the game you will see these symbols associated with the state. Without even trying terribly hard to memorize the facts, they will begin to just seep into your brain!

Crossword Puzzles

Follow crossword instructions on page 14, using the state name for clues and state capital for answers.

Musical States and Capitals

Audio tapes and CDs help you learn the states and capitals. Play them in the car, while doing chores, preparing dinner, taking a bath, or doing the dishes. States and Capitals Songs cassette and CD from Audio Memory covers the states in geographical order from "northern border of the United States...," "...the middle of the United States...," and so on. Another audio, called States and Capitals, is by Twin Sisters Productions. It uses excellent quality music to help you learn state information and capitals by putting words to familiar patriotic tunes.

Geography Through Art

It is fascinating to include art with any study of geography. Artistic students or those who learn well with crafts and hands-on activities benefit from the lessons in *Teaching Geography Through Art* by Rich and Sharon Jeffus. Look for art projects from this book listed on the appropriate *POINTS OF INTEREST* pages.

Recommended **Trail Blazing** resources:
- Trail Guide to U.S. Geography Student Notebook CD-ROM or eBook
- *Uncle Josh's Outline Map Book* or CD-ROM (if you do not have the Student Notebook)
- *Children's Illustrated Atlas of the United States*
- Geography Terms Chart - for defining geography terms
- *Teaching Geography Through Art*
- *Eat Your Way Through the USA*
- 3-ring binder and dividers - for State Notebook
- Almanac, library books, encyclopedia, or other research resources
- Reproducible sheets from the appendix
- Colored pencils

Geography Through Literature

The Lewis and Clark Expedition

During the final six weeks of this course, students travel with Lewis and Clark's Corps of Discovery and explore northern parts of the Louisiana Purchase in search of the Northwest Passage while reading the novel *The Captain's Dog, My Journey with the Lewis and Clark Tribe* by Roland Smith. Written from the perspective of Meriweather Lewis's dog, Seaman, and true to real events, this exciting narrative includes excerpts from Lewis's personal journal.

Students map the route as they read through the book. Additional assignments include learning about the various Indian tribes, geography, vocabulary, plants, and animals of the expedition. Weekly reading assignments can be spread out through the week or read in one sitting. It is highly recommended that you read aloud if possible. Use questions to help assess comprehension, as a springboard for discussion, and more. For your convenience, suggested answers are provided in parentheses after each question. (More detailed instructions can be found beginning on page 112.)

Recommended Literature resources:
- *The Captain's Dog, My Journey with the Lewis and Clark Tribe* by Roland Smith (Gulliver Books Harcourt, Inc., ISBN:0-15-202696-7)
- United States outline map (*Uncle Josh's Outline Map Book* or CD-ROM)
- *Children's Illustrated Atlas of the United States*
- Colored pencils
- Library books or other research resources

Optional:
U.S. historical atlas with the Lewis and Clark route marked
U.S. road atlas (for finding places along the Missouri River where Lewis and Clark traveled)
National Geographic Feb. 2003 issue (great article on Sacajawea and the expedition)

Trail Guide to U.S. Geography
Sample Schedule

These general weekly schedules are provided as a guide. Adapt them to fit your needs. Use more or less time depending upon student skill level and abilities. Make a "Face the Facts" chart the first week of each new region to use as a reference the following week(s). This is a five-day plan, but feel free to use this curriculum for only four days a week.

One state a week

Monday
- 5-minute drills
- 15 minutes on memorization (capitals, abbreviations, etc. of region)
- Geography terms

Tuesday
- 5-minute drills
- 15-20 minutes on mapping

Wednesday
- 5-minute drills
- 20-30 minutes on simple Trail Blazing projects

Thursday
- 5-minute drills
- 20-30 minutes reading and researching choice of Trail Blazing projects

Friday
- 30-45 minutes on writing final copy of any Trail Blazing report, an art project from *Geography Through Art,* or any Trail Blazing project which may take more time

Two states a week

Monday
- 5-minute drills
- 15-20 minutes on mapping first state
- 15-20 minutes Trail Blazing same state

Tuesday
- 5-minute drills
- 30-40 minutes on more Trail Blazing projects

Wednesday
- 5-minute drills
- 15-20 minutes on mapping second state
- 15-20 minutes Trail Blazing second state

Thursday
- 5-minute drills
- 30-40 minutes on Trail Blazing projects of second state

Friday
- 15 minutes on memorization (capitals, abbreviations, etc. of region)
- Geography terms
- Art project or complete any unfinished Trail Blazing projects

Co-op groups or classroom
Each student must have access to his own atlas for answering the questions and for completing the mapping assignments. Give a variety of Trail Blazing assignments to different students and let all share what they have learned with the group.

Join our Yahoo user group:
http://groups.yahoo.com/group/geographytrailguides

18

NEW ENGLAND STATES

Maine

Massachusetts

New Hampshire

Vermont

Connecticut

Rhode Island

GEOGRAPHY TRAILS
Week 1 - New England States

Day 1

What is the capital of Maine? What country is north of Maine?

What is Maine's state bird? Name one river in Maine that flows into the Atlantic Ocean.

What is the land area of Maine? Maine's chief agricultural crop is grown in the north; what is it?

Day 2

What mountains make up the central part of Maine? Maine's jagged coastline is longer than California's; what ocean forms the boundary of this coastline?

What river flows from Moosehead Lake to the Atlantic Ocean? What is the only state that touches Maine?

From what two cities in Maine could you depart on an international airline flight? What national park is located at the Atlantic Ocean?

Day 3

What is the capital of Massachusetts? What two states lie on Massachusetts' northern border?

Where in Massachusetts are the Berkshire Hills located? What river flows into Boston Bay?

What is the general climate of Massachusetts? What is the state motto of Massachusetts?

Day 4

In what bay will you find Massachusetts' capital city? What Massachusetts cape juts into the Atlantic Ocean?

What five states border Massachusetts? What is the highest point in Massachusetts?

What is Massachusetts' nickname? Name five rivers in Massachusetts.

POINTS OF INTEREST

Maine

Mapping

- Draw and label Kennebec River.
- Label Canada, New Hampshire, and Atlantic Ocean.
- Label Augusta with a star.

- Shade and label the Appalachian, Katahdin, and Blue Mountains.
- Shade and label Chamberlain, and Chiputneticook lakes.
- Label Kennebunk and Bar Harbor.

- Place a brown triangle at Mount Katahdin and label its name and elevation.
- Draw and label St. John, St. Croix, Kennebec, and Penobscot rivers.
- Shade and label Moosehead and Sebago lakes.
- Label Canada, New Hampshire, and the Atlantic Ocean.
- Label Augusta, Portland, Eastport, Fort Kent, and Bangor.

Trail Blazing

As a Matter of Fact...

In order to eliminate a navigational hazard in the Kennebec River (at Augusta) the people of Maine once hitched 200 oxen to Cushnoc Island in a failed attempt to move the island. Add this and any other interesting "Matter of Fact" to your notebook.

> **Geography Terms**
> hill
> cape

Read about Maine's name, state symbols, and motto. Tell what you learned.

Study the coast of Maine. Learn what industries the many miles of coastline and salt water support. Compare its length when measured in a straight line from border to border to its actual length of curvy, zigzagging coast.

Learn about Maine's oldest lighthouse, Portland Head Light. Write a journal entry as a lighthouse keeper in the 1800s during a harrowing storm. Include a picture of a lighthouse in your notebook. Compare lighthouses in the 1700s to those in use today.

Maine has an abundance of pine forests, making it a major producer of lumber and other wood products. List some of the products manufactured in Maine.

Maine supplies about half of the country's lobster. Learn what conditions are required for lobsters to live. How are they caught and transported to the rest of the U.S.? Include a picture of a lobster in your notebook.

Name some famous people from Maine and what they accomplished. Choose one person to write about and include it in your notebook, or copy one of Henry Wadsworth Longfellow's poems in your notebook.

Begin to learn the capitals of all states in this region.

Make a timeline of Maine starting in 1607 when English settlers first established Popham Colony.

Select from the list of state projects on page 121.

POINTS OF INTEREST

Massachusetts

Mapping

- Draw and label Connecticut and Charles rivers.
- Label New York, Vermont, New Hampshire, Rhode Island, Connecticut, and Atlantic Ocean.
- Label Boston with a star.

- Label Buzzards Bay, Cape Cod Bay, Boston Bay, and Massachusetts Bay.
- Label Cambridge, Salem, and Amherst.

- Shade and label the Berkshire Hills.
- Place a brown triangle at Mount Greylock and label its name and elevation.
- Shade and label Quabbin Reservoir.
- Draw and label Merrimack, Connecticut, Concord, and Charles rivers.
- Label Cape Cod, Nantucket Sound, Martha's Vineyard, and Nantucket Island.
- Label Boston, Concord, Plymouth, and Lexington.

Trail Blazing

As a Matter of Fact...

One of the first incidents of the Revolutionary War, the Battle of Bunker Hill, actually took place on Breed's Hill. Add this and any other interesting "Matter of Fact" to your notebook.

> **Geography Terms**
> hill
> cape

Read about Massachusetts' name, state symbols, and motto. Tell what you learned.

Read about the rich history of Massachusetts and list a few of its many "firsts."

Learn what Native Americans lived in Maine when the Europeans settled there. Write or tell about the relationship between the colonists and Indians.

Study the Plymouth Plantation and learn about the trials faced by the Pilgrims there. Include a quote from William Bradford's diary or copy the Mayflower Compact in your notebook.

Copy or draw a diagram or map of the streets of Boston that make up the Freedom Trail. Include the historic sites along the trail.

Study the Industrial Revolution and how it affected the lives of the factory workers. Explain the changes associated with the emergence of the textile mills and factories and increased availability of goods.

Read about the geography, climate, and natural resources of Massachusetts. Tell how each of these are related to one another and how they affect the state's economy.

Name some famous people from Massachusetts and what they accomplished. Choose one person to write about and include it in your notebook, or copy a poem by Emily Dickinson in your notebook.

Make a timeline of Massachusetts starting in 1498 when John Cabot first explored the coast.

Select from the list of state projects on page 121.

GEOGRAPHY TRAILS
Week 2 - New England States

Day 1

What ocean forms part of the boundary of New Hampshire? What is New Hampshire's state bird?

Name four cities in New Hampshire that lie along the Merrimack River. When it is noon in Denver, CO, what time is it in New Hampshire's state capital? (hint: see time zone map in appendix.)

Does New Hampshire's topography include low rolling coast, hills and mountains, or plateau? What are New Hampshire's chief industries?

Day 2

What river flows along the east of Concord, New Hampshire's capital city? What country is north of New Hampshire?

What is the highest point in New Hampshire? What northern New Hampshire lake crosses the boundary into Maine?

What is the total land area of New Hampshire? What contributes to New Hampshire's varied climate?

Day 3

What mountain range runs north and south through Vermont? What state forms the southern boundary of Vermont?

What lake forms the northwest boundary of Vermont? What is the only New England state without a seacoast?

Which state has more square miles of land area, Vermont or New Hampshire? Name three chief crops of Vermont.

Day 4

What lake forms part of Vermont's east boundary with New York? What is the capital of Vermont?

What river flows through the small town of Middlebury, Vermont? The West River flows from Vermont into what state?

Use one word to describe the terrain of Vermont. What forms the 20-35-mile-wide backbone running north and south through Vermont?

POINTS OF INTEREST

New Hampshire

Mapping

- Draw and label Connecticut and Merrimack rivers.
- Label Canada, Maine, Atlantic Ocean, Massachusetts, and Vermont.
- Label Concord with a star.

- Shade and label the White Mountains.
- Shade and label Umbagog Lake.
- Shade and label the Franklin Falls Reservoir.

- Place a brown triangle at Mount Washington and label its name and elevation.
- Shade and label Winnipesaukee Lake.
- Draw and label the Connecticut, Merrimack, and Pemigewasset rivers.
- Label Canada, Maine, Atlantic Ocean, Massachusetts, and Vermont.
- Label Concord, Portsmouth, Manchester, and Nashua.

Trail Blazing

As a Matter of Fact…

The windiest place on earth is atop Mount Washington. Add this and any other interesting "Matter of Fact" to your notebook.

Read about New Hampshire's name, state symbols, and motto. Tell what you learned.

> **Geography Terms**
> mountain range
> bridge

New Hampshire has thriving manufacturing and tourist industries. Read about the geography, climate, and natural resources. Tell how each of these are related to one another and how they affect the state's economy.

New Hampshire is a major producer of granite. List the uses for granite and explain how it is quarried.

The Old Man of the Mountain was one of the world's most notable natural features until recently (May 2003) when it was destroyed by erosion. Find out its size and of what kind of rock it was formed. Locate a picture of it before and after its demise for inclusion in your notebook.

Name some famous people from New Hampshire and what they accomplished. Choose one person to write about and include it in your notebook, or copy a poem by Robert Frost in your notebook.

New Hampshire was the first colony to adopt its own constitution. Study New Hampshire's political and governmental history. Compare the number of representatives in New Hampshire's State House to that of other states. Explain why the nation focuses on the presidential primary elections there.

Learn the two-letter postal abbreviation of all states in this region.

Make a timeline of New Hampshire starting in 1603 when European Martin Pring explored the territory.

Select from the list of state projects starting on page 121.

Week 2   24   New England

POINTS OF INTEREST

Vermont

Mapping

- Draw and label Connecticut and Merrimack rivers.
- Label Canada, New York, Massachusetts, and New Hampshire.
- Label Montpelier with a star.

- Shade and label the Green Mountains.
- Shade and label Memphremagog Lake.

- Place a brown triangle at Mount Mansfield and label its name and elevation.
- Shade and label Champlain Lake.
- Draw and label the Connecticut River.
- Label Canada, New York, Massachusetts, and New Hampshire.
- Label Montpelier.

Trail Blazing

As a Matter of Fact...

If you attended a performance at the Haskell Opera House at Derby Line, you would sit in the state of Vermont, U.S.A., and watch performers on stage in Canada. Add this and any other interesting "Matter of Fact" to your notebook.

Read about Vermont's name, state symbols, and motto. Tell what you learned.

Vermont is the only New England state without a seacoast. Describe the land and how its location makes Vermont different from the other New England states.

Vermont is the country's leading producer of maple syrup. Sap from four trees, about 40 gallons, is boiled down to produce one gallon of maple syrup. Learn more about the production of maple syrup. Use pure maple syrup on your pancakes this week or sweeten lemonade with maple syrup instead of sugar.

Vermont is a major producer of marble and has the largest granite quarries in the U.S. Read about the geography, climate, and other natural resources. Tell how each of these are related to one another and how they affect the state's economy.

Learn about Vermont's town meetings. Write a newspaper article about a town meeting.

Read about Ethan Allen and the Green Mountain Boys and their contribution to the Revolutionary War. Write or tell about what you learned.

Name some famous people from Vermont and what they accomplished. Choose one person to write about and include it in your notebook, or Include one of Norman Rockwell's pictures in your notebook.

Make a timeline of Vermont starting in 1609 when Samuel de Champlain claimed the land for France.

Select from the list of state projects starting on page 121.

GEOGRAPHY TRAILS
Week 3 - New England States

Day 1

🐾 What is Connecticut's state capital? What three states form Connecticut's boundary on its north, east, and west sides?

🐾 What river flows through Connecticut's state capital? Name two rivers that flow into Long Island Sound.

🐾 What are the chief ports of Connecticut? Describe the climate in Connecticut.

Day 2

🐾 Which Connecticut river is farther south: Quinnipiac, Thames, or Housatonic? What is Connecticut's state tree?

🐾 Is 60% of Connecticut covered in forests, mountains, or plains? What is Connecticut's highest point?

🐾 What are two of the chief manufactured goods in Connecticut? What is the state motto of Connecticut?

Day 3

🐾 What large body of water is south of Rhode Island? What is the highest point in Rhode Island?

🐾 The western part of Rhode Island is made up of many islands; name one. What are the two main rivers in Rhode Island?

🐾 Where does Rhode Island rank in land area in the 50 states? Describe the topography of Rhode Island.

Day 4

🐾 What island is located in the Atlantic Ocean, south of Rhode Island? What is the capital of Rhode Island?

🐾 How wide is Rhode Island at its widest point? What Rhode Island bay is home to numerous offshore islands?

🐾 The first permanent settlement in America was founded at what city in 1636? What are the chief industries in Rhode Island?

POINTS OF INTEREST

Connecticut

Mapping

- Draw and label Connecticut River.
- Label Massachusetts, Rhode Island, and New York.
- Label Hartford with a star.

- Label Long Island Sound.
- Shade and label Lake Candlewood.
- Draw and label Saugatuck, Farmington, Shetucket, Thames, and Quinebaug rivers.

- Place a brown triangle at Mount Frissel and label its name and elevation.
- Shade and label Mansfield Hollows Lake
- Draw and label Housatonic and Connecticut rivers.
- Label Massachusetts, Rhode Island, and New York.
- Label Hartford, New Haven, and Bridgeport.

Trail Blazing

As a Matter of Fact...

In the 1700s Lime Rock metal workers forged a huge chain with three-foot long links. It was stretched across the Hudson River to prevent British ships from sailing up the strategic waterway during the American Revolution. Add this and any other interesting "Matter of Fact" to your notebook.

> **Geography Terms**
> bay
> island

Read about Connecticut's name, state symbols, and motto. Tell what you learned.

Connecticut manufactures clocks, computers, aircraft parts, helicoptors, and submarines. Read about the geography, climate, and natural resources. Tell how each of these are related to one another and how they affect the state's economy.

Learn the story of the Charter Oak. Retell it to your classmates or family.

Sixty percent of the state is forest land. Learn what kinds of trees make up the forests. Make a list of the trees and include pictures in your notebook.

Name some famous people from Connecticut and what they accomplished. Choose one person to write about and include it in your notebook, or copy a famous quote from Nathan Hale in your notebook.

Eli Whitney introduced mass production when he manufactured muskets with interchangeable parts. Learn about mass production and how its inception changed the way goods were produced from the early 1800s.

Work on memorizing the capitals of the New England states and the Mid-Atlantic states by using flash cards, playing the concentration game, or by making a crossword puzzle.

Make a timeline of Connecticut starting in 1614 when Adriaen Block first explored the area.

Select from the list of state projects on page 121.

POINTS OF INTEREST

Rhode Island

Mapping

- Label Massachusetts, Connecticut, and Atlantic Ocean.
- Label Providence with a star.

- Draw and label Scituate Reservoir.
- Label Rhode Island Sound and Block Island Sound.
- Label Narragansett Bay

- Place a brown triangle at Jerimoth Hill and label its name and elevation.
- Draw and label Blackstone, Wood, and Queen rivers.
- Label Massachusetts, Connecticut, and Atlantic Ocean.
- Label Providence, Newport, and Pawtucket.

Trail Blazing

As a Matter of Fact…

The official name of Rhode Island is the longest of all other states: The State of Rhode Island and Providence Plantations. Add this and any other interesting "Matter of Fact" to your notebook.

Read about Rhode Island's name, state symbols, and motto. Tell what you learned.

Roger Williams established the first settlement in Providence in 1636 after he was exiled from the Massachusetts Bay Colony. Anne Hutchinson settled Portsmouth in 1638 while in exile. Learn the stories behind these two people and write an "If you were there" type of newspaper article about the culture of the times.

Read about the Great Swamp Fight of 1675 and in what war it was fought. Tell what you learned.

Rhode Island is a major producer of textiles and jewelry. Read about the geography, climate, and natural resources. Tell how each of these are related to one another and how they affect the state's economy.

Samuel Slater built America's first water-powered spinning jenny in 1790. Learn about the spinning jenny and its impact on the textile industry in Rhode Island. Write about what you learned.

Newport is known for its mansions originally built as summer homes in the 1800s. Read about some of these mansions and include pictures in your notebook. Include the mansion names, who built them, why and when they were built.

Learn the two-letter postal abbreviation of all states in this region.

Make a timeline of Rhode Island starting in 1524 when Giovanni da Verrazzano first explored the Narragansett Bay.

Select from the list of state projects on page 121.

Week 3

New England

MID-ATLANTIC STATES

New York
New Jersey
Pennsylvania
West Virginia
Maryland
Delaware

GEOGRAPHY TRAILS
Week 4 - Mid-Atlantic States

Day 1

What state is north of Pennsylvania? What is the capital of West Virginia?

What capital city is located on the Delaware River? In what state are both the Adirondack Mountains and Catskill Mountains located?

What is the rank by population of the state of New York? What fruits are among the chief crops grown in New York?

Day 2

What lake forms much of the northern border of New York? What mountains span the eastern U.S. and run through the Mid-Atlantic states?

What bay forms the southwestern boundary of New Jersey? New Jersey is connected to mainland U.S. only by its shared boundary with what state?

What percent of the land in New York is forested? (See formula hint on student reference sheet page 121.) What three cities are home to chief ports in New York?

Day 3

What river flows north and south through eastern New York, passing by the capital city? What states share a boundary with Delaware?

Which of the five Great Lakes forms part of Pennsylvania's boundary? What is the name of the large area of pine, oak, and cedar forest land in southern New Jersey?

What are the chief industries of New Jersey? What physical geography covers three-fifths of the state of New Jersey?

Day 4

What state has Annapolis for its capital city? What river forms the border between New Jersey and Pennsylvania?

What long narrow body of water separates Long Island, NY, from the U.S. mainland? What is the highest point in the Mid-Atlantic Region?

Which state has the highest per capita income: Pennsylvania, New Jersey, or New York? What kind of lumber is grown in New Jersey?

POINTS OF INTEREST

New York

Mapping

- Draw and label the Hudson River.
- Label Pennsylvania, Canada, Vermont, New Jersey, Massachusetts, Connecticut, and the Atlantic Ocean.
- Label Albany with a star.

- Shade and label the Adirondack, Catskill, and Appalachian Mountains.
- Shade and label the Finger Lakes, and Lake Champlain.
- Draw and label the Susquehanna, Delaware, and Gennessee rivers.

- Place a brown triangle at Mount Marcy and label its name and elevation.
- Shade and label Lake Ontario and Lake Erie.
- Draw and label the St. Lawrence, Niagara, and Hudson rivers.
- Label Long Island, and Long Island Sound.
- Label Pennsylvania, Canada, Vermont, Massachusetts, Connecticut, New Jersey, and the Atlantic Ocean.
- Label Albany, New York City, West Point, Rochester, Buffalo, and Syracuse.

Trail Blazing

As a Matter of Fact...

New York City passed the world's first speed limit law in 1652. Add this and any other interesting "Matter of Fact" to your notebook.

Read about New York's name, state symbols, and motto. Tell what you learned.

> **Geography Terms**
> review

New York is the world center of finance and tourism. Read about the geography, climate, and natural resources. Tell how each of these are related to one another and how they affect the state's economy.

New York City has a population of over seven million, which is higher than 39 of the 50 states. Make a population density map of the United States.

Write a report on Niagara Falls. Include its size, annual number of visitors, who owns it, and how many gallons of water fall per minute. Include a human interest story of accidents or incidents at the falls.

Learn about the Statue of Liberty. Of what is it made, who made it, and how was it transported to its location? Write out the inscription found on its base and explain its meaning. What is its significance to immigration and the growth of our nation?

The Erie Canal, a waterway dug in eight years without modern technology, was completed in 1825. It connected New York City with Buffalo, New York. Find out how this transportation route affected trade between states and the economy as a whole. Trace the history from its opening to its use today.

Make a timeline of New York starting in 1524 when Verrazzano first sailed into New York Bay.

Select from the list of state projects on page 121.

Geography Through Art
Statue of Liberty

POINTS OF INTEREST

New Jersey

Mapping

- Draw and label the Hudson River.
- Label New York, Pennsylvania, Delaware, and Atlantic Ocean.
- Label Trenton with a star.

- Shade and label the Pine Barrens and the Coastal Plain.
- Shade and label Lake Hopatcong.
- Label Great Bay and Barnegat Bay.
- Label Princeton.

- Place a triangle at High Point and label its name and elevation.
- Draw and label the Hudson and Delaware rivers.
- Label Raritan Bay and Delaware Bay.
- Label New York, Pennsylvania, Delaware, and Atlantic Ocean.
- Label Trenton, Atlantic City, and Jersey City.

Trail Blazing

As a Matter of Fact...

The inventions of Thomas Edison helped make New Jersey the motion picture capital of the world (until about 1916). Add this and any other interesting "Matter of Fact" to your notebook.

Read about New Jersey's name, state symbols, and motto. Tell what you learned.

New Jersey is a leader in the chemistry industry and in scientific/industrial research and claims to have the greatest variety of manufactured products. Read about the geography, climate, and natural resources. Tell how each of these are related to one another and how they affect the state's economy.

While New Jersey is the most densely populated state in the U.S., it still has many truck farms, orchards, and green houses. Learn what crops are grown there.

Write a newspaper account of the destruction of the *Hindenburg* at Lakehurst in 1937. Include where it was going, where its fateful journey began, how many were killed, and how many survived. Gather information on how dirigibles work, and include a summary in your newspaper article.

Name some famous people from New Jersey and what they accomplished. Choose one person to write about and include it in your notebook, or copy one of Walt Whitman's poems in your notebook.

Study Thomas Edison, and list some of his many inventions.

Retell the story of how George Washington led his soldiers across the Delaware River at night to a surprise victory during one of the nearly 100 Revolutionary War battles fought in New Jersey.

Make a timeline of New Jersey starting in 1524 when Verrazzano first sailed along the coast.

Select from the list of state projects on page 121.

GEOGRAPHY TRAILS
Week 5 - Mid-Atlantic States

Day 1
What state is north of Delaware? What is the capital of Pennsylvania?

What river flows into the Atlantic Ocean near Staten Island and Long Island, NY? Is West Virginia's Allegheny Plateau located east or west of the Appalachian Mountains?

What is the general climate of Pennsylvania? Where are the chief ports in Pennsylvania?

Day 2
What ocean is east of New Jersey? What river flows through Washington, D.C.?

What West Virginia gorge is known as the Grand Canyon of the East? What is the highest point in Pennsylvania?

What kinds of livestock contribute to Pennsylvania's economy? What is Pennsylvania's rank by population?

Day 3
What is the state bird of West Virginia? What bay nearly divides Maryland in two?

What river flows through Pennsylvania's state capital? What is the state nickname of West Virginia?

What physical terrain covers two-thirds of the state of West Virginia? Is the per capita income of West Virginia higher or lower than the per capita income of Virginia?

Day 4
Name all states that share a boundary with Pennsylvania. What is the state tree of West Virginia?

Name two reservoirs in Pennsylvania. Until the Civil War, West Virginia was part of what state?

What are the chief goods manufactured in West Virginia? What trees grown in West Virginia are used for lumber?

33

POINTS OF INTEREST

Pennsylvania

Mapping

- Draw and label the Susquehanna and Delaware rivers.
- Label New York, New Jersey, Delaware, Maryland, West Virginia, Ohio, and Lake Erie.
- Label Harrisburg with a star.

- Shade and label the Appalachian Mountains.
- Shade and label the Allegheny Reservoir and Pymatuning Reservoir.

- Place a brown triangle at Mount Davis and label its name and elevation.
- Draw and label the Susquehanna, Allegheny, and Delaware rivers.
- Label New York, New Jersey, Delaware, Maryland, West Virginia, Ohio, and Lake Erie.
- Label Harrisburg, Philadelphia, Pittsburgh, and Erie.

Trail Blazing

As a Matter of Fact...

At Lake Pymatuning sometimes the carp swim so closely together that ducks walk across their backs. Add this and any other interesting "Matter of Fact" to your notebook.

Read about Pennsylvania's name, state symbols, and motto. Tell what you learned.

> **Geography Terms**
> chasm
> mine

All of the hard coal in the U.S. is mined in Pennsylvania. Learn about coal, its uses, mining procedures, and land reclamation.

Write a report on Philadelphia, home of Independence Hall (the site of the signing of the Declaration of Independence and the U. S. Constitution), the Liberty Bell, Carpenter's Hall, Benjamin Franklin's print shop, and more.

Gettysburg was the site of one of the bloodiest battles of the Civil War in July of 1863. The Union win served as a turning point for the war. President Lincoln gave his famous Gettysburg Address when he dedicated a part of the battlefield as a cemetery. Copy the Gettysburg Address for your notebook.

Name some famous people from Pennsylvania and what they accomplished. Choose one person to write about and include it in your notebook, or make a list of books written by Louisa May Alcott.

Pennsylvania is home to Mennonite and Amish people, some of whom still speak Pennsylvania Dutch, a variation of German. Learn about how their religion affects their lifestyle.

Make a timeline of Pennsylvania starting in 1608 when Captain John Smith is first known to have visited the area.

Select from the list of state projects on page 121.

Geography Through Art
- Pennslyvania Dutch Design/American Folk Art
- Fractur

POINTS OF INTEREST

West Virginia

Mapping

- Draw and label the Ohio river.
- Label Kentucky, Ohio, Pennsylvania, Maryland, and Virginia.
- Label Charleston with a star.

- Shade and label the Allegheny Plateau and the Appalachian Mountains.
- Draw and label the Kanawha and Cheat rivers.

- Place a triangle at Spruce Knob and label its name and elevation.
- Draw and label the New, Potomac and Ohio, rivers.
- Label Kentucky, Ohio, Pennsylvania, Maryland, and Virginia.
- Label Charleston, Wheeling, and Parkersburg.

Trail Blazing

As a Matter of Fact...

Located in the narrow "panhandle" of West Virginia, Weirton is the only city in the U.S. that stretches from the border of one state to the border of another. Add this and any other interesting "Matter of Fact" to your notebook.

Read about West Virginia's name, state symbols, and motto. Tell what you learned.

West Virginia was admitted to the Union during the Civil War. Learn how and why.

West Virginia suffered tremendously during the Civil War. One town changed hands over 50 times. Write a story about a Civil War battle in West Virginia.

Most of the west-central part of West Virginia lies over vast natural gas fields. Learn about how natural gas and bituminous coal supports the economy of West Virginia. Study the state's industries, natural resources, location, and weather. Tell how each of these are related to one another and how they affect the state's economy.

The New River Gorge is known as the Grand Canyon of the East and holds the longest steel arch bridge in the world (near Hinton). The bridge is 1700 feet long, and, at 876 feet above the gorge, is the second highest bridge in the U.S. Learn about steel arch bridges. Make a list of the locations of other bridges of this kind.

There are over 200 natural hot springs in West Virginia. Learn how they are formed, what keeps them hot, and the therapeutic uses for hot springs. Make an advertisement brochure for an imaginary hot springs spa company.

Review states and capitals of the New England states and Mid-Atlantic states.

Make a timeline of West Virginia starting in 1669 when John Lederer explored the region.

Select from the list of state projects on page 121.

GEOGRAPHY TRAILS
Week 6 - Mid-Atlantic States

Day 1
What state is east of Pennsylvania? What is the capital of New York?

A canal in northern Delaware is named for the two bodies of water it connects; what is its name? What two bays are located in southeast Delaware?

What are the chief crops of Maryland? What is Maryland's state flower?

Day 2
To what state does Long Island belong? What river forms the north and west boundary of West Virginia?

What is the land area of Delaware and its rank by area? Located in Maryland, what is the largest bay in the U.S.?

What is the climate in the eastern part of Maryland? Is the per capita income of Maryland higher or lower than the per capita income of Maine?

Day 3
What is the state bird of Delaware? What is the two-letter postal abbreviation for Maryland?

The Mason-Dixon line is the boundary between what two states? Although Washington, D.C. is not located in any state, it is surrounded by the boundaries of what state?

What is the topography of Delaware? What is the climate of Delaware?

Day 4
What is the capital of Delaware? Into what bay does the Delaware River flow?

If a person living in Maryland called his friend in Phoenix, AZ, what time would he need to place the call to interrupt his friend's dinner at 6 P.M.? What is the highest point in Maryland?

What percentage of the land area of Delaware is forested? (See formula hint on student reference sheet page 121.) Is the population density of Delaware less than 400 people per square mile or more than 400 people per square mile?

POINTS OF INTEREST

Maryland

Mapping

- Draw and label the Potomac River.
- Label the Chesapeake Bay.
- Label Pennsylvania, Delaware, Virginia, West Virginia, and the Atlantic Ocean.
- Label Annapolis with a star.

- Shade and label the Allegheny Mountains.
- Label Cambridge.

- Place a brown triangle at Backbone Mountain and label its name and elevation.
- Draw and label the Patuxent and Potomac rivers.
- Label the Chesapeake Bay.
- Draw a square to identify the land area of the nation's capital, Washington, D.C, and shade it in yellow.
- Label Annapolis, Baltimore, and Cumberland.

Trail Blazing

As a Matter of Fact…

Maryland's width near Hancock, at one mile wide, is the narrowest of any state. Add this and any other interesting "Matter of Fact" to your notebook.

Read about Maryland's name, state symbols, and motto. Tell what you learned.

The Chesapeake Bay, the largest estuary in the United States, provides about half of the nation's blue crab harvest each year. The bay contains mostly salt water from the Atlantic Ocean but also receives fresh water from the rivers that flow into the bay. This region attracts a wide variety of migratory birds and is home to over 2700 species of plants and animals. Describe an estuary and make a list of seafood products from Maryland.

> **Geography Terms**
> estuary
> canal

Study Baltimore and learn about its impact as a port city. Tell how it is different from most other port cities. (Hint: look at the location of Baltimore.)

Washington, D.C. became the U. S. capital in 1800. Both Maryland and Virginia contributed land for the territory. Write a report on the history of Washington, D.C., its planning, and construction. Explain the difference between a U.S. district and a U.S. state. Include pictures or drawings of some of the buildings and sites.

Name some famous people from Maryland and what they accomplished. Choose one person to write about and include it in your notebook, or copy in your notebook the lyrics written by Frances Scott Key that became our national anthem.

Make a timeline of Maryland starting in 1608 when Captain John Smith first explored Chesapeake Bay.

Select from the list of state projects on page 121.

Geography Through Art
Washington Monument

POINTS OF INTEREST

Delaware

Mapping

- Draw and label the Chesapeake and Delaware Canal.
- Label Pennsylvania, Maryland, New Jersey, and Atlantic Ocean.
- Label Dover with a star.

- Draw and label the Nanticoke River.
- Label Rehoboth Bay and Indian River Bay.
- Label Milford and Newark.

- Place a brown triangle at the highest point in New Castle County and include the elevation.
- Draw and label the Delaware and Mispillion rivers.
- Draw and label the Chesapeake and Delaware Canal.
- Label the Delaware Bay.
- Label Dover and Wilmington.

Trail Blazing

As a Matter of Fact...

Pea Patch Island was formed as a result of a shipwreck. When the ship carrying peas wrecked on a sandbar, the peas rooted and grew, gathering so much sand that the birth of an island ensued. Add this and any other interesting "Matter of Fact" to your notebook.

Read about Delaware's name, state symbols, and motto. Tell what you learned.

Some of Delaware's industries include chemicals, agriculture, and finance. Read about the geography, climate, and natural resources. Tell how each of these are related to one another and how they affect the state's economy.

Scandinavian settlers introduced the log cabin to the colonies. Since forests provided an abundant supply of logs, the log cabin quickly became a standard American style of home. Read about log cabin construction and write or tell about what you learned.

Despite its small size, more corporations are based in Delaware than in any other state. Find out why.

Learn about the du Pont family of Delaware and what they accomplished. Write a report and include it in your notebook along with a picture of the Winterthur Museum.

Read about the Great Sand Hill. Find out how this landmark was formed and how tall it is.

Review states and capitals of this region by using flash cards, making a crossword puzzle, or playing Concentration.

Make a timeline of Delaware starting in 1609 when Henry Hudson first sailed the Half Moon up the Delaware Bay.

Select from the list of state projects on page 121.

GEOGRAPHY TRAILS
Week 7 - Review

Day 1

🐾 What Maine river flows between the Katahdin Mountains and the Blue Mountains? What is the postal abbreviation for Vermont?

🐾 What two states are located at Connecticut's northeast corner? List the following states in order by area from largest to smallest: New Jersey, Vermont, Maryland, and New Hampshire.

🐾 Which Mid-Atlantic state uses the most square miles of land for agriculture? Which New England states have land north of 45°N latitude?

Day 2

🐾 What is the Massachusetts state bird? What ocean forms the southern border of Connecticut?

🐾 In what time zone is Pittsburgh, PA, located? The New York Barge Canal passes through Rochester, NY; is Rochester north or south of Lake Ontario?

🐾 Which Mid-Atlantic state has the lowest sales tax? Which Mid-Atlantic state has the largest Hispanic population?

Day 3

🐾 What is the state tree of Massachusetts? What is the capital of New Jersey?

🐾 What Mid-Atlantic state is actually a peninsula? What state has a partially rounded border – an arc at twelve miles distance from New Castle?

🐾 Which state has the highest commercial fishing income: New Hampshire, Maine, or Connecticut? Is the population density of Boston, MA, more than 10,000, or less than 10,000 people per square mile?

Day 4

🐾 What is the postal abbreviation for Maryland? What mountain range is located along the border of West Virginia and Pennsylvania?

🐾 What two rivers meet to form the Ohio River? Are the Berkshire Hills located in the eastern or western part of Massachusetts?

🐾 What is the zip code of Newport, VT? How many counties comprise the state of Connecticut?

POINTS OF INTEREST

Review

No new assignments.

Use this week to complete any unfinished projects. Make sure you know the following from memory of all states you have studied up to now:

- state capitals
- postal abbreviations
- location - be able to identify each state on an outline map of the U.S.

Organize your State Notebook.

SOUTHERN STATES

North Carolina
Virginia
Kentucky
Tennessee
South Carolina
Georgia
Alabama
Mississippi
Florida
Arkansas
Louisiana

GEOGRAPHY TRAILS

Week 8 - Southern States

Day 1

🐾 What is the capital of Virginia? What state is south of North Carolina?

🐾 What two bodies of water surround the Delmarva Peninsula of Virginia? What is the highest point in Virginia, and where is it located?

🐾 What are the high and low altitudes of North Carolina, and where are they? How many miles of Atlantic Ocean coastline does Virginia have?

Day 2

🐾 What body of water forms the coastline of Georgia? What river forms the boundary between South Carolina and Georgia?

🐾 What national park is located at the border between North Carolina and Tennessee? What is the name of the area of rolling land east of North Carolina's Blue Ridge Mountains?

🐾 About how many miles long and wide is the state of Virginia? (hint: states, U.S., area) Which state produces more bushels of corn, North Carolina or South Carolina? (hint: agriculture)

Day 3

🐾 What is the state bird of North Carolina? Raleigh is the capital of what state?

🐾 Name two large lakes southeast of the capital city of South Carolina. What state is located southwest of South Carolina?

🐾 Is the American Indian population of North Carolina more than or less than 100,000? What is the annual precipitation in Asheville, NC?

Day 4

🐾 The Blue Ridge Mountains are the east and southeast range of what mountains? What state lies north of North Carolina?

🐾 What is the highest point in Georgia, and where is it located? What river carries water from both the Oconee River and Ocmulgee River into the Atlantic Ocean at St. Simon's Island, GA?

🐾 What is the highest recorded temperature in Virginia, and when was it recorded? Describe Virginia's climate.

POINTS OF INTEREST

North Carolina

Mapping

- Draw and label Cape Fear River.
- Label Virginia, Tennessee, Georgia, South Carolina, and Atlantic Ocean.
- Label Raleigh with a star.

- Shade and label the Blue Ridge Mountains and the Piedmont.
- Shade and label Lake Norman, High Rock Lake, and Kerr Lake.
- Label Cape Hatteras, Cape Lookout, and Cape Fear.

- Place a brown triangle at Mount Mitchell and label its name and elevation.
- Draw and label Roanoke, Cape Fear, and Neuse rivers.
- Label Albemarle Sound and Pamlico Sound.
- Shade and label the Great Smoky Mountain National Park in green.
- Label Virginia, Tennessee, Georgia, South Carolina, and Atlantic Ocean.
- Label Raleigh, Kitty Hawk, Charlotte, and Asheville.

Trail Blazing

As a Matter of Fact...

Throw a handkerchief across the ridge of Blowing Rock, a unique natural formation, and it will come back on its own from the current of air below. Add this and any other interesting "Matter of Fact" to your notebook.

Read about North Carolina's name, state symbols, and motto. Tell what you learned.

> **Geography Terms**
> piedmont
> plateau

Study the geography of North Carolina. Notice three distinctive regions: coastal plains, piedmont, and mountains. Shade your map three different colors for these three regions and add them to a legend. Notice the differences in climate and natural resources in each region. Consider how they relate to one another and how they affect the state's economy.

The Outer Banks is the name given to the line of barrier islands on North Carolina's east coast. This area has shallow waters, reefs, and shoals. Read about the Outer Banks and its rich history. Some topics of interest: shipwrecks, Blackbeard, the Lost Colony of Roanoke Island, the Wright brothers' famous first flight, and Cape Hatteras Lighthouse (tallest brick lighthouse) Write or tell about what you learned.

The Research Triangle is a nearly 7000-acre park established in 1959 as a place for research for business and industry. Learn more about the Research Triangle, where it is located, and make a list of some of the companies that conduct research there.

Begin to memorize the states and capitals of this region making flash cards, playing Concentration, or making a crossword puzzle.

Make a timeline of North Carolina starting in 1524 when Giovanni da Verrazzano explored the coast.

Select from the list of state projects on page 121.

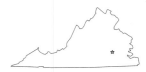

POINTS OF INTEREST

Virginia

Mapping

Υ Υ
- Draw and label the Potomac River.
- Label Maryland, West Virginia, Kentucky, Tennessee, North Carolina, and Atlantic Ocean.
- Label Richmond with a star.

🐾
- Shade and label the Appalachian and Blue Ridge Mountains.
- Label the Chesapeake Bay and the Delmarva Peninsula.

🐾🐾
- Place a brown triangle at Mount Rogers and label its name and elevation.
- Draw and label York, Potomac, Roanoke, James, and Shenandoah rivers.
- Label Richmond, Virginia Beach, Arlington, Lynchburg, Norfolk, and Williamsburg.

Trail Blazing

As a Matter of Fact...
Virginia extends so far west (as far as Detroit, Michigan) that it might be considered a midwestern state. Add this and any other interesting "Matter of Fact" to your notebook.

> **Geography Terms**
> hill
> cape

Read about Virginia's name, state symbols, and motto. Tell what you learned.

 Read about Virginia's geography, climate, and natural resources. Tell how each of these relate to one another and how they affect the state's economy.

The Natural Bridge is a stone bridge over which Virginia's Route 11 passes. It has an interesting history. Learn about this bridge; find out who once owned it and how big it is. Write a short report for your notebook.

Virginia is known as the mother of Presidents. List all eight presidents born in Virginia.

The land for Arlington National Cemetery once belonged to Robert E. Lee. Learn about this world-famous cemetery and write a summary to include in your notebook. Include pictures if possible.

Virginia is one of three states that form the Delmarva Peninsula - the land between the Chesapeake Bay and the Atlantic Ocean. From its name, take a guess at what other two states have land forming this peninsula.

Name some famous people from Virginia and what they accomplished. Choose one person to write about and include it in your notebook, or copy Patrick Henry's famous quote in your notebook.

Make a timeline of Virginia starting in 1607 when English settlers founded Jamestown.

Select from the list of state projects on page 121.

GEOGRAPHY TRAILS
Week 9 - Southern States

Day 1

What is the two-letter postal abbreviation for Kentucky? What is the capital of Tennessee?

What Kentucky national park is home to the longest cave system in the world? Is the land in Kentucky mostly desert, plains, mountainous, or hilly?

How many federal hazardous waste sites are located in Kentucky? Which of these southern states has the lowest production of crude oil: Alabama, Arkansas, or Kentucky? (hint: oil production)

Day 2

What man-made lake located in both Kentucky and Tennessee provides electricity? What mountain range runs along Tennessee's eastern boundary and North Carolina's western boundary?

What plateau runs along the Tennessee River west of the Appalachian Mountains? What is the highest point in Tennessee, and in what national park is it located?

In Kentucky, which of these crops produce the greatest annual yield: corn, soybeans, or tobacco? (hint: agriculture) What are the high and low elevations in Tennessee, and where are they?

Day 3

What is Virginia's state tree? What is the postal abbreviation for North Carolina?

What is the land area of North Carolina and its rank by area? What cape is located south of Kitty Hawk, NC?

What is the lowest recorded temperature in Kentucky, and when was it recorded? In what month does Nashville, TN, normally receive the highest precipitation? (hint: weather)

Day 4

What river forms the northern boundary of Kentucky? What is the state bird of Virginia?

What three rivers, originating in Virginia, flow into the Chesapeake Bay? What national park is located in the northern part of Virginia?

Which two states have about the same number of farms: North Carolina and South Carolina, or Kentucky and Tennessee? (hint: agriculture) Which state has a lower average price of eggs: Tennessee, Kentucky, or Virginia? (hint: agriculture)

POINTS OF INTEREST

Kentucky

Mapping

ΨΨ
- Draw and label the Ohio River.
- Label Ohio, West Virginia, Virginia, Tennessee, Missouri, Illinois, and Indiana.
- Label Frankfort with a star.

- Shade and label the Appalachian Mountains.
- Shade and label Mammoth Cave National Park in green.
- Draw and label the Cumberland River.
- Label Somerset.

- Place a brown triangle at Black Mountain and label its name and elevation.
- Shade and label Lake Barkley, Kentucky Lake, and Lake Cumberland.
- Draw and label Ohio, Mississippi, and Kentucky rivers.
- Label Ohio, West Virginia, Virginia, Tennessee, Missouri, Illinois, and Indiana.
- Label Frankfort, Louisville, Lexington, Fort Knox, and Paducah.

Trail Blazing

As a Matter of Fact…

Perhaps the world's only moonbow can be seen at Kentucky's Cumberland Falls at midnight in the spring and summer. Add this and any other interesting "Matter of Fact" to your notebook.

> **Geography Terms**
> review

Read about Kentucky's name, state symbols, and motto. Tell what you learned.

Daniel Boone blazed the Wilderness Trail through the Cumberland Gap. This trail became the main route for settlers traveling west. Draw the route of the Wilderness Trail on an outline map of the U.S.

Mammoth Cave is the longest cave system in the world. Learn about caves, how they are formed and from what types of rock. Define stalactite and stalagmite. Learn how cave-dwelling animals are different from those who live above ground.

The Shakers, an innovative religious group, settled in Kentucky in the early 1800s. Learn more about the Shakers, their lifestyle, and how they got their name; list some of the useful items they created. Study the Shaker furniture style and determine what design features identify furniture as Shaker.

Fort Knox is one of the premier military training centers in the world. It is also the site of the federal gold depository, where over $6 billion of gold bullion is stored. Read about Fort Knox, and tell what you have learned. Include a picture of Ft. Knox in you notebook.

Name some famous people from Kentucky and what they accomplished. Choose one person to write about and include it in your notebook, or copy a quote or story told by Abraham Lincoln in your notebook.

Make a timeline of Kentucky starting in 1654 when Virginia Colonel Abram Wood first explored it.

Select from the list of state projects on page 121.

Geography Through Art
- Basket Weaving
- Pioneer Doll

POINTS OF INTEREST

Tennessee

Mapping

- Draw and label the Tennessee River.
- Label Kentucky, Virginia, North Carolina, Georgia, Alabama, Mississippi, Arkansas, and Missouri.
- Label Nashville with a star.

- Shade and label the Appalachian Mountains, Cumberland Plateau, and Great Smoky Mountains.
- Shade and label Chickamauga Lake.
- Shade Tennessee's three distinctive land regions: (1) eastern mountains, brown; (2) central rolling land, orange; and (3) the western lowlands between the Tennessee and Mississippi Rivers, green.

- Place a brown triangle at Clingman's Dome and label its name and elevation.
- Shade and label Kentucky and Norris lakes.
- Draw and label the Tennessee, Cumberland, and Mississippi rivers.
- Label Nashville, Memphis, Chattanooga, and Knoxville.

Trail Blazing

As a Matter of Fact...

The greatest variety of birds in the U. S. is in Tennessee. Add this and any other interesting "Matter of Fact" to your notebook.

Read about Tennessee's name, state symbols, and motto. Tell what you learned.

Tennessee's economy is supported in part by the chemical industry and transportation equipment. Read about the geography, climate, and natural resources. Tell how each of these are related to one another and how they affect the state's economy.

In 1933 Congress created the Tennessee Valley Authority to control flooding, improve navigation, and generate electricity through a series of dams along the Tennessee River. Learn more about the TVA.

"Be always sure you're right, then go ahead" was the motto of Davy Crockett. Read about this frontiersman and storyteller and add the information to your notebook.

Read about the Cherokee Indian nation and the "Trail of Tears." Tell about what you learned.

Memphis is a transportation hub for the shipping industry. Explain the impact of the Mississippi River on this industry and describe other transportation resources used in Memphis.

Study the music industry and how Nashville, TN, plays a role. What is Nashville's nickname, and what famous country music facility is in Nashville?

Make a timeline of Tennessee starting in 1540 when Hernando de Soto led the first white expedition.

Select from the list of state projects on page 121.

GEOGRAPHY TRAILS
Week 10 - Southern States

Day 1
What is the capital of South Carolina? What state is south of Georgia?

What is the highest point in South Carolina, and where is it located? What is the area of South Carolina and its rank by area?

Georgia is ranked seventh in the U.S. for nonfuel mineral production; what are the principal minerals produced in Georgia? (hint: mineral production) Does South Carolina produce more or less tobacco than Kentucky?

Day 2
What is the two-letter postal abbreviation for Georgia? Which state does NOT have mountains: Georgia, South Carolina, or Florida?

If you were on vacation in beautiful Savannah, GA, and wanted to call your grandmother in Los Angeles, CA, what time would you need to call to reach her at noon? At what river is the Walter F. George Reservoir?

About how many miles wide and long is the state of Georgia? (hint: states, U.S., area) Which of these southern states produces more cotton: Georgia, Louisiana, or South Carolina?

Day 3
What is Georgia's state bird? What river flows along the western boundary of Georgia?

Where are the Florida Keys? What two national parks are located in southern Florida?

Place these states in order by soybean production from greatest to least: Georgia, Florida, and South Carolina. What is the highest recorded temperature in North Carolina, and when was it recorded?

Day 4
What is the state tree of South Carolina? Is Lake Murray located in the eastern, western, or central part of South Carolina?

What body of water connects Lake Kissimmee to Lake Okeechobee? St. Petersburg, FL, is located at what bay?

What is the average annual precipitation of South Carolina? North Carolina is the only southern state in the top ten for Native American population; what is its rank? (hint: population, Native American)

POINTS OF INTEREST

South Carolina

Mapping

- Draw and label Savannah River.
- Label North Carolina, Georgia, and Atlantic Ocean.
- Label Columbia with a star.

- Shade and label the Blue Ridge Mountains and the Piedmont.
- Shade and label Lake Keowee and Lake Murray.
- Label Hilton Head Island.
- Label Sumter and Greenville.

- Place a brown triangle at Sassafras Mountain and label its name and elevation.
- Shade and label Lake Marion and Lake Moultrie.
- Draw and label Savannah, Great Pee Dee, and Lynches rivers.
- Label North Carolina, Georgia, and Atlantic Ocean.
- Label Columbia, Charleston, and Myrtle Beach.

Trail Blazing

As a Matter of Fact…

South Carolina was the site of more Revolutionary War battles than any other state. Add this and any other interesting "Matter of Fact" to your notebook.

> **Geography Terms**
> sandbar
> dock

Read about South Carolina's name, state symbols, and motto. Tell what you learned.

South Carolina is a leader in producing vermiculite and glass fiber. Its textile belt runs through Spartanburg and Greenville. Read about the geography, climate, and natural resources. Tell how each of these are related to one another and how they affect the state's economy.

Nearly one-fourth of workers in South Carolina have jobs making textiles. Study the textile industry.

More Revolutionary War battles were fought on the land that became South Carolina than in any other state. Read about the Revolutionary War and what significant battles were won and lost in South Carolina.

Slaves were once sold at the Old Slave Mart in Charleston. Learn about slavery and conditions on the slave ships that landed in the Charleston harbor.

Learn about Francis Marion, known as the "Swamp Fox," and his contribution to the Revolutionary War. Include a short summary in your notebook.

Learn the two-letter postal abbreviation of all states in this region.

Make a timeline of South Carolina starting in 1521 when Francisco Gordillo first explored its coast.

Select from the list of state projects on page 121.

POINTS OF INTEREST

Georgia

Mapping

- Draw and label Chattahoochee River.
- Label South Carolina, North Carolina, Tennessee, Alabama, Florida, and Atlantic Ocean.
- Label Atlanta with a star.

- Shade and label the Appalachian Mountains.
- Shade and label Lake Sinclair, Lake Seminole, Lake Oconee, and Walter F. George Reservoir.

- Place a brown triangle at Brasstown Bald and label its name and elevation.
- Shade and label Lake Sidney Lanier and West Point Lake.
- Draw and label Chattahoochee, Savannah, Oconee, Altamaha, and Flint Rivers.
- Label South Carolina, North Carolina, Florida, Tennessee, Alabama, and Atlantic Ocean.
- Label Atlanta, Savannah, Macon, and Augusta.

Trail Blazing

As a Matter of Fact...

Sometimes disputes between Cherokee and Creek Indians were settled by a ball game. Add this and any other interesting "Matter of Fact" to your notebook.

> **Geography Terms**
> hill
> cape

Read about Georgia's name, state symbols, and motto. Tell what you learned.

Georgia is the leading transportation center of the Southeast. Read about the geography, climate, and natural resources. Tell how each of these are related to one another and how they affect the state's economy.

Georgia farmers produce over 1.5 billion pounds of peanuts annually. Learn what kind of soil and climate conditions are needed to grow them, and find out the various uses for peanuts. Write a short summary of your study of peanuts and include the contribution of George Washington Carver to its history.

The cotton gin was invented in Georgia by Eli Whitney. Read about the history of the cotton industry. Explain how cotton is harvested, prepared, and used. Describe the kind of climate needed to grow cotton. Write a summary of your study.

Nearly one-half of the state's population lives in the metropolitan Atlanta area. Make a travel brochure of Atlanta and include favorite tourist stops.

Read about Martin Luther King Jr. and how his life impacted the civil rights movement in America. Copy a quote from his famous "I Have a Dream" speech in your notebook.

Begin to memorize the Southern states and their capitals by using flash cards, playing Concentration, or making a crossword puzzle.

Make a timeline of Georgia starting with the expedition led by Hernando de Soto in 1540.

Select from the list of state projects on page 121.

GEOGRAPHY TRAILS
Week 11 - Southern States

Day 1

❧❧ What state is east of Mississippi? What three states form the southern boundary of Tennessee?

🐾 What is the highest point in Arkansas, and where is it located? What state is located at the south-west corner of Arkansas?

🐾 Does Alabama produce more or less crude oil than Mississippi? Which state uses more acreage for farming: Alabama, Arkansas, or Mississippi?

Day 2

❧❧ What is the capital of Arkansas? What gulf forms the southern boundary of Louisiana, Mississippi, and Alabama?

🐾 What is the largest lake in Louisiana? Would you expect Louisiana's northern or southern region to have the lower elevation? (Explain why.)

🐾 What are the average high and low temperatures in Alabama in January? Do Alabama farmers produce more bushels of corn, soybeans, or wheat yearly?

Day 3

❧❧ What is the two-letter postal abbreviation for Arkansas? Is Lake Pontchartrain in Alabama or Louisiana?

🐾 What is the highest point in Alabama, and where is it located? What Alabama bay is located at the Gulf of Mexico?

🐾 Are there more American Indians living in Mississippi or in Alabama? Is the average price of a dozen eggs in Mississippi higher or lower than in Connecticut?

Day 4

❧❧ What is the state bird of Louisiana? What state forms the northern boundary of Arkansas?

🐾 What river flows through Ross Barnett Reservoir and forms part of the boundary between Mississippi and Louisiana? What is the area of Mississippi and its rank by area?

🐾 With only 44 miles of coastline, Mississippi has one of the top 25 busiest ports in America; where is it located? During what month does Jackson, MS, receive the most average precipitation?

POINTS OF INTEREST

Alabama

Mapping

- Draw and label Alabama River.
- Label Tennessee, Mississippi, Florida, Georgia, and Gulf of Mexico.
- Label Montgomery with a star.

- Shade and label the Appalachian Mountains.
- Shade and label Wheeler, Weiss, Guntersville lakes.
- Draw and label Tombigbee, Black, and Warrior, rivers.

- Place a brown triangle at Cheaha Mountain and label its name and elevation.
- Shade and label Lake Martin and Lake Eufaula.
- Draw and label Alabama, Tallapoosa, Tennessee, and Chattahoochee rivers.
- Label Mobile Bay.
- Label Tennessee, Mississippi, Florida, Georgia, and Gulf of Mexico.
- Label Montgomery, Mobile, Huntsville, and Tuscaloosa.

Trail Blazing

As a Matter of Fact...

The first rocket to land a man on the moon was built in Huntsville. Add this and any other interesting "Matter of Fact" to your notebook.

Read about Alabama's name, state symbols, and motto. Tell what you learned.

> **Geography Terms**
> elevation
> reservoir

Alabama has over 1300 miles of waterways, providing an abundant opportunity for shipping goods. Learn about Mobile's seaport and what goods enter and leave the country from this location.

Read about Alabama's geography, climate, and natural resources. Tell how each of these are related to one another and how they affect the state's economy.

Learn how the culture of America changed after Rosa Parks refused to give up her seat in the bus in Montgomery in 1955. Make a Civil Rights timeline depicting the events that followed her arrest.

Huntsville is the site of the world's largest space museum and home to Space Camp, a hands-on interactive camp for adults and children interested in true-to-life space mission training. Call or write for a brochure about Space Camp. (U.S. Space & Rocket Center, One Tranquility Base, Huntsville, AL, 35805-3399, 1-800-637-7223)

Name some famous people from Alabama and what they accomplished. Choose one person to write about and include it in your notebook.

Make a timeline of Alabama starting in 1519 when Alonso Alvarez de Pineda arrived in Mobile Bay.

Select from the list of state projects on page 121.

Week 11

Southern

POINTS OF INTEREST

Mississippi

Mapping

- Draw and label Mississippi River.
- Label Louisiana, Arkansas, Tennessee, Alabama, and the Gulf of Mexico.
- Label Jackson with a star.

- Shade and label the Yazoo Basin, Black Prairie, and Pine Hills.
- Shade and label Grenada Lake, Pickwick Lake, and Ross Barnett Reservoir.

- Place a brown triangle at Woodall Mountain and label its name and elevation.
- Draw and label Big Black, Yazoo, Tombigbee, and Mississippi rivers.
- Label Louisiana, Arkansas, Tennessee, Alabama, and the Gulf of Mexico.
- Label Jackson, Biloxi, Gulfport, Greenville, Natchez, and Vicksburg.

Trail Blazing

As a Matter of Fact…

The Pascagoula River has been nicknamed the Singing River because it sometimes makes the sound of humming bees. This phenomenon has never been explained. Add this and any other interesting "Matter of Fact" to your notebook.

Read about Mississippi's name, state symbols, and motto. Tell what you learned.

Read about Mississippi's geography, climate, and natural resources. Tell how each of these are related to one another and how they affect the state's economy.

Learn about the boll weevil and its impact upon the history of Mississippi agriculture.

Learn more about the Mississippi River. Write a short report. Include its contribution to the nation's transportation and economy.

Cotton seeds were first brought to the U.S. in the 1500's by Spanish explorers. Learn about Mississippi's cotton plantations and how the Civil War affected the cotton industry. Study cotton and its uses.

The discovery of oil in 1939 brought industrialization to Mississippi. List the key industries of this state.

Name some famous people from Mississippi and what they accomplished. Choose one person to write about and include it in your notebook.

Make a timeline of Mississippi starting in 1540 when Hernando de Soto explored the Mississippi.

Select from the list of state projects on page 121.

Geography Through Art
Antebellum architecture

GEOGRAPHY TRAILS
Week 12 - Southern States

Day 1

What area of water lies within the curved coastline formed by the states of Texas, Louisiana, Mississippi, Alabama, and Florida? The southernmost part of the Appalachian Mountains is in the eastern part of what state?

What city is located at approximately 30°N 90°W? The Tombigbee River crosses the border between what two states?

Which state has more percentage of federally owned land: Alabama, Florida, or Georgia? Does Florida have more coastline on the Gulf of Mexico or on the Atlantic?

Day 2

The Chattahoochee River forms a boundary between what two states? The Mississippi River delta is in what state?

What is the land area of Florida? What bay is located at approximately 30°N 84°W?

Where is Florida's busiest port? (hint: port traffic) What are the chief industries that support Florida's economy?

Day 3

What is the two-letter postal abbreviation for Florida? What is the state bird of Alabama?

Is Sarasota, FL, on the Gulf coast or the Atlantic coast of Florida? The panhandle of Florida is south of what state?

Which state has more hazardous waste sites: Alabama, Florida, or Mississippi? Florida is ranked 5th in U.S. nonfuel mineral production; what minerals are produced there?

Day 4

What large lake is located in the central part of Florida between Fort Myers and West Palm Beach? Is the capital of Florida closer to Orlando or Jacksonville?

Into what harbor does the Peace River in Florida empty? What is the highest point in Louisiana, and where is it located?

Do travelers to Florida spend more than $50 billion or less than $50 billion annually? Which state produces more crude oil: Florida, Georgia, or Tennessee?

POINTS OF INTEREST

Florida

Mapping

- Draw and label Suwanee River.
- Label Georgia, Alabama, Mississippi, Atlantic Ocean, and Gulf of Mexico.
- Label Tallahassee with a star.

- Draw and label St Mary's, Peace, and Perdido rivers.
- Label Florida Keys, Charlotte Harbor, Tampa Bay, Whitewater Bay, and Sanibel Island.
- Label Pensacola, Panama City, Jacksonville, and Key West.

- Place a brown triangle at the highest peak in Walton County and label with the elevation.
- Shade and label Lake George, Lake Kissimmee, and Lake Okeechobee.
- Draw and label St. John's, Suwanee, and Apalachicola rivers.
- Label Georgia, Alabama, Mississippi, Atlantic Ocean, and Gulf of Mexico.
- Label Tallahassee, Tampa, St. Petersburg, Orlando, Daytona Beach, Cape Canaveral, and Miami.

Trail Blazing

As a Matter of Fact...

When the anhinga (water turkey) are finished fishing, they lie on the beach with outstretched wings to dry their feathers - appearing much like laundry left out to dry. Add this and any other interesting "Matter of Fact" to your notebook.

> **Geography Terms**
> peninsula
> swamp

Read about Florida's name, state symbols, and motto. Tell what you learned.

St. Augustine is the oldest continuously inhabited European settlement in North America. Obtain travel brochures on St. Augustine and learn about its rich history.

Read about Florida's produce industry and its tourism. Which provides more income to the state? Learn how Florida's weather, location, and natural resources are related. Find out how the opening of Disney World in Orlando affected tourism and the economy.

Florida has one of the lowest average elevations of all the states. Learn about the Florida Everglades and list the animal and plant life that thrives there.

The first American in orbit (John Glenn) lifted off in the *Friendship Seven* spacecraft at Cape Canaveral. Read about NASA and the space program in Florida. Include a summary in your notebook.

In 1912 the first railroad from Miami to Key West was built with bridges that extended from island to island. Read about the railroad construction, bridge building, and promoter Henry Flagler.

Make a timeline of Florida starting in 1513 when Ponce de Leon first explored it.

Select from the list of state projects on page 121.

GEOGRAPHY TRAILS
Week 13 - Southern States

Day 1

What river flows through Little Rock, AR, and into the Mississippi River? What two states lie across the Mississippi River from the state of Mississippi?

Lake Pontchartrain Causeway is the longest highway bridge in the world; in what state is it located? What city, located southeast of Baton Rouge, LA, is known for its annual Mardi Gras festival?

Does Arkansas produce more bushels of soybeans, corn, or wheat? About how many miles wide and long is the state of Arkansas? (hint: states, U.S., area)

Day 2

In what state are the Ozark Mountains, Boston Mountains, and Ouachita Mountains located? If you crossed the Mississippi River from Memphis, TN, in what state would you end up?

If you crossed the Mississippi River at Lake Providence, LA, in what state would you arrive? From what state does the Mississippi River spill into the Gulf of Mexico?

What is the lowest elevation in Arkansas, and where is it? What is the average annual precipitation in Arkansas as measured in North Little Rock?

Day 3

What river lies east of the Cumberland Plateau? What river flows south out of Kentucky Lake?

What state shares Mississippi's northwest boundary? What is the highest point in Mississippi, and in what corner of the state is it located?

What is the total Gulf of Mexico coastline of Louisiana compared to the shoreline? Which state produces more corn: Louisiana, Alabama, or Georgia?

Day 4

What river flows from Kentucky through Nashville, TN, and back into Kentucky again? What is the capital of Louisiana?

What is the largest Tennessee city located on the Mississippi River? Is the mountaneous region in Tennessee east or west of Nashville?

What is the elevation at the lowest point in Louisiana, and where is it located? Which state produces more crude oil: Alabama, Arkansas, or Louisiana?

POINTS OF INTEREST

Arkansas

Mapping

- Draw and label Arkansas River.
- Label Missouri, Tennessee, Mississippi, Louisiana, Texas, and Oklahoma.
- Label Little Rock with a star.

- Shade and label the Ozark, Boston, and Ouchita Mountains.
- Shade and label Great Ferry Lake, Blue Shoals Lake, Norfolk Lake, and Dardenelle Lake.

- Place a brown triangle at Magazine Mountain and label its name and elevation.
- Shade and label Lake Ouchita.
- Draw and label Arkansas, White, Mississippi, and St. Francis rivers.
- Label Missouri, Tennessee, Mississippi, Louisiana, Texas, and Oklahoma.
- Label Little Rock, Fort Smith, and Hot Springs.

Trail Blazing

As a Matter of Fact...

America's only diamond mine is located near Murfreesboro, where visitors can hunt for and keep all diamonds they find. Add this and any other interesting "Matter of Fact" to your notebook.

> **Geography Terms**
> review

Read about Arkansas's name, state symbols, and motto. Tell what you learned.

Over 70,000 diamonds have been unearthed in volcanic fields near Murfreesboro. Learn about the diamond industry in Arkansas and its impact on the economy.

Read about Arkansas's geography, climate, and natural resources. Tell how each of these are related to one another and how they affect the state's economy.

Over 47 separate hot springs in the Ouachita Mountains release about one million gallons of steaming water daily. Learn what causes the over 140° water to be released from the earth's surface. Write or tell what you learned.

Steamboats that can operate in a foot of water were developed so they could be used in the many shallow rivers in Arkansas. Read about steam engines. Write a summary about what you learned.

Arkansas produces more rice than any other state. Learn about rice farming techniques. Make a list of the steps for growing rice.

Review the states and capitals of this region by using flash cards, working a crossword puzzle, or by playing Concentration.

Make a timeline of Arkansas starting in 1541 when Hernando de Soto crossed the Mississippi into what is now Arkansas.

Select from the list of state projects on page 121.

POINTS OF INTEREST

Louisiana

Mapping

- Draw and label Mississippi River.
- Label Texas, Arkansas, Mississippi, and the Gulf of Mexico.
- Label Baton Rouge with a star.

- Place a brown triangle at Driskill Mountain and label its name and elevation.
- Shade and label Sabine, Calcasieu, and Grand lakes.
- Label Toledo Bend Reservoir and Atchafalaya Bay.

- Shade and label Lake Pontchartrain.
- Draw and label Red, Atchafalaya, Mississippi, and Pearl rivers.
- Label Texas, Arkansas, Mississippi, and the Gulf of Mexico.
- Label Baton Rouge, New Orleans, and Shreveport.

Trail Blazing

As a Matter of Fact...

New Orleans, built on the silt of the Mississippi River, is sinking; about two-thirds of the city lies eight feet below sea level. Add this and any other interesting "Matter of Fact" to your notebook.

> **Geography Terms**
> delta
> bayou

Read about Louisiana's name, state symbols, and motto. Tell what you learned.

Learn what industries contribute to the economy of Louisiana. Read about the geography, climate, and natural resources. Tell how each of these are related to one another and how they affect the state's economy.

Jazz music, said by some to be the only art form to originate in America, first developed in Louisiana in the late 1800s. Learn what distinguishes jazz from other forms of music. Make a list of some famous jazz musicians and what instruments are typically used in jazz.

America's busiest port is outside of New Orleans. Read about the Port of South Louisiana: its size, the number of oceangoing vessels that pass through yearly. Make a list of what goods leave the port.

Read about the difference between Creole and Cajun and list some influences of both to the culture and traditional foods of Louisiana.

Lake Pontchartrain Causeway spans nearly 24 miles and is the longest highway bridge in the world. Read about how and when this bridge was built and if was damaged by Hurricane Katrina in August 2005. Write about what you learned and include a picture or drawing in your notebook.

Name some famous people from Louisiana and what they accomplished. Choose one person to write about and include it in your notebook.

Make a timeline of Louisiana starting in 1541 with Hernando de Soto's expedition.

Select from the list of state projects on page 121.

GEOGRAPHY TRAILS
Week 14 - Review

Day 1

What body of water forms the western boundary of Florida? What mountain range is located west of Little Rock, AR?

In what North Carolina geographic region are most of the people and industry located? The Research Triangle is located amid what three North Carolina cities?

Which state had the highest population in 1790? Which state had the highest population in 1890?

Day 2

What is the Kentucky state tree? What North Carolina river flows through Wilmington and empties into the Atlantic Ocean?

What Kentucky city hosts the Kentucky Derby, one of the most famous horse races in the world? What southern state produces more rice than any other state?

Which three southern states* have the lowest amount of federally-owned acreage? (hint: land, federally owned) Which state is larger by area: North Carolina, Georgia, or Florida?

Day 3

Is New Orleans the capital of Louisiana? What is the postal abbreviation of Virginia?

The Great Smoky Mountains National Park attracts the most visitors; in what state(s) is it located? The goober is the top product grown in Georgia; what is a goober?

Which state does NOT have a tropical or subtropical climate: Louisiana, Kentucky, or Tennessee? Which state has the highest violent crime rate: Virginia, Georgia, or Arkansas?

Day 4

What river forms part of the boundary between Alabama and Georgia? What is the capital of Mississippi?

Which state has more historical sites than any other, including the homes of Presidents Washington and Jefferson? If you drove 400 miles due north from Atlanta, what capital city would you be near?

What two southern states have less than 50% of forested land? Does the United States export or import more commodities?

*For states in the south, see map on pages 6 or 41.

POINTS OF INTEREST

Review

No new assignments.

Use this week to complete any unfinished projects. Make sure you know the following from memory of all states you have studied up to now:

- state capitals
- postal abbreviations
- location - be able to identify each state on an outline map of the U.S.

Organize your State Notebook.

MIDWESTERN STATES

Ohio   Iowa

Indiana   North Dakota

Wisconsin   Nebraska

Michigan   Missouri

Illinois   South Dakota

Minnesota   Kansas

GEOGRAPHY TRAILS
Week 15 - Midwestern States

Day 1

What state is east of Indiana? What river forms the boundary between Ohio and the states of Kentucky and West Virginia?

Into what river does the Ohio River empty? What state is on Ohio's northwest boundary?

What is the topography of Ohio? What are the chief crops of Ohio?

Day 2

Is the capital of Michigan located on the Upper Peninsula or Lower Peninsula? What is the state nickname for Michigan?

What land area forms the northern boundary of Lake Michigan? What land area forms the northern boundary of Lake Superior?

Does Ohio produce more crude oil than South Dakota? Which city has more average annual precipitation: Columbus, OH, or Detroit, MI?

Day 3

What is the two-letter postal abbreviation for Ohio? What state is made up of two peninsulas?

At which of the Great Lakes is Michigan's Saginaw Bay located? Michigan is made up of two bodies of land nearly surrounded by water; what is this geographical formation called?

Which Michigan city has the lowest mean temperature in January: Detroit, Grand Rapids, or Marquette? In which state are eggs the least expensive: Illinois, Indiana, or Michigan?

Day 4

What Great Lake forms the northern boundary of Ohio? Columbus is the capital of what state?

What strait is located between Michigan's Upper Peninsula and Lower Peninsula? What is Ohio's state nickname?

Does Michigan have more or less farmland than Indiana? What are Michigan's chief ports?

POINTS OF INTEREST

Ohio

Mapping

- Draw and label Ohio River.
- Label Michigan, Indiana, Kentucky, West Virginia, and Pennsylvania.
- Label Columbus with a star.

- Place a brown triangle at Campbell Hill and label it with name and elevation.
- Shade and label Lake Erie.
- Draw and label Scioto, Maumee, Muskingum, and Ohio rivers.
- Label Columbus, Toledo, Cincinnati, Cleveland, and Dayton.

Trail Blazing

As a Matter of Fact...

The first professional baseball team in America was the Cincinnati Red Stockings. Add this and any other interesting "Matter of Fact" to your notebook.

> **Geography Terms**
> review

Read about Ohio's name, state symbols, and motto. Tell what you learned.

Ohio's abundance of minerals makes it one of the country's most important manufacturing states. Learn what kinds of products are manufactured there and why. Include the importance of Ohio's water sources and how water contributes to the economy.

Read about Ohio's geography, climate, and natural resources. Tell how each of these are related to one another and how they affect the state's economy.

Settlers first arrived in Ohio from the east by floating on flatboats down the Ohio River. Learn more about Ohio's history, taking note of how water played an important role in transportation. Find out how the Ohio River was used in the winter by the Underground Railroad.

Name some famous people from Ohio and what they accomplished. Choose one person to write about and include it in your notebook. You might want to include some interesting inventors or their inventions, such as the hot dog or floating soap (Ivory), or make a list of some of Thomas Edison's inventions.

Read about the Mound Builders and the Great Serpent Mound. Write or tell what you learned.

Begin to memorize the states and capitals of this region through making flash cards, playing Concentration, or making a crossword puzzle.

Make a timeline of Ohio starting in 1669 when Robert Cavalier Sieur de La Salle claimed the entire region west of the Alleghenies for France.

Select from the list of state projects on page 121.

POINTS OF INTEREST

Michigan

Mapping

- Draw and label Muskegon River.
- Shade and label Lake Superior, Lake Huron, Lake Erie, and Lake Michigan.
- Label Indiana, Ohio, Wisconsin, and Canada.
- Label Lansing with a star.

- Shade and label the Copper Range (Porcupine Mountains).
- Shade and label Lake St. Clair.
- Draw and label Saginaw River.
- Label Keweenaw Peninsula, Straits of Mackinac, Saginaw Bay, and Thunder Bay.

- Place a brown triangle at Mount Arvon and label it with name and elevation.
- Shade and label Lake Superior, Lake Huron, Lake Erie, and Lake Michigan.
- Draw and label Kalamazoo, Muskegon, and Manistee rivers.
- Label Indiana, Ohio, Wisconsin, and Canada.
- Label Lansing, Battle Creek, Grand Rapids, Detroit, and Sault Sainte Marie.

Trail Blazing

Geography Terms
dell
waterfall

As a Matter of Fact…

Michigan has the greatest variety of trees of all the states. Add this and any other interesting "Matter of Fact" to your notebook.

Read about Michigan's name, state symbols, and motto. Tell what you learned.

Michigan is the nation's largest producer of automobiles, salt, mint, navy beans, and sour cherries. Read about the geography, climate, and natural resources. Tell how each of these are related to one another and how they affect the state's economy.

Breakfast cereals were invented as a special health food diet by John Kellogg in Battle Creek. Read about Kellogg and his brother and their contributions to revolutionizing how that first meal of the day is served.

Mackinac Island (pronounced mackinaw) is a famous resort island. Make a travel brochure telling about what makes it unique.

Name some famous people from Michigan and what they accomplished. Choose one person to write about and include it in your notebook.

Henry Ford introduced the assembly line, method to automobile production and completely revolutionized transportation. Study the history of the automobile and what contribution Ford's methods made to the common man.

Michigan is the only state made up of two distinctly different land masses - two peninsulas. List how these two regions are different in climate, culture, and natural resources.

Make a timeline of Michigan starting in 1620 when Etienne Brulé explored the Upper Peninsula.

Select from the list of state projects on page 121.

GEOGRAPHY TRAILS
Week 16 - Midwestern States

Day 1
What states border Lake Michigan? What four Great Lakes form a coastline along Michigan?

What two rivers converge at the southwestern tip of Indiana, and where do they empty? Indiana's steel mills and oil refineries are located near which of the five Great Lakes?

Which Indiana city has a higher population density: Indianapolis or Fort Wayne? Which county in Indiana has the largest area, and which county has the highest population?

Day 2
If you crossed the Wabash River heading west from Indiana, in what state would you land? What three bodies of water form part of Illinois's boundary?

What body of water is at Illinois's northeast border, and what "Windy City" is located there? What Illinois city is across the Missouri River from St. Louis, MO?

What percentage of the total land area in Indiana is forested? What is the general climate of Indiana?

Day 3
What is the capital of Indiana? What river flows through Terre Haute and forms part of Indiana's western boundary?

In what direction is Illinois's state capital from Chicago? What are the land area and rank by area of Illinois?

What are the latitude and longitude coordinates for Peoria, Illinois? Illinois produces more corn than all other states except which one?

Day 4
What is the state bird of Indiana? Is Chicago the capital of Illinois?

What states border Lake Superior? In what city is the annual 500-mile auto race run on Memorial Day weekend?

What are the lowest temperature and highest temperature recorded in Chicago, IL? What is the general topography of Illinois?

POINTS OF INTEREST

Indiana

Mapping

YY
- Draw and label Ohio River.
- Shade and label Lake Michigan.
- Label Michigan, Ohio, Kentucky, and Illinois.
- Label Indianapolis with a star.

🐾🐾
- Place a brown triangle at the highest point in Wayne County and label with the elevation.
- Shade and label Lake Michigan, Shafer, Lake Monroe, and Patoka Lake.
- Draw and label Kankakee, Tippecanoe, Wabash, White, and Ohio rivers.
- Label Michigan, Ohio, Kentucky, and Illinois.
- Label Indianapolis, Evansville, Gary, Fort Wayne, Kokomo, and South Bend.

> **Geography Terms**
> cultivated land
> field

Trail Blazing

As a Matter of Fact...

Santa Claus, Indiana, (zip code 47579) receives half a million pieces of mail to re-mail with the town's post mark every Christmas season. Add this and any other interesting "Matter of Fact" to your notebook.

Read about Indiana's name, state symbols, and motto. Tell what you learned.

Indiana is the largest steel producer of any state. Learn about steel production and where in Indiana this industry thrives. Make a list of products made from steel.

🐾 Indiana produces more dimensional limestone than any other state. Read about the geography, climate, and natural resources. Tell how each of these are related to one another and how they affect the state's economy.

Indiana limestone has been used on the Empire State Building, the Pentagon, and many other important structures. Read about limestone mining and what geologic conditions produce limestone.

No one knows why residents of Indiana are called Hoosiers. There are many stories attempting to explain the term's origin. See how many stories you can find and tell them to your family.

Name some famous people from Indiana and what they accomplished. Choose one person to write about and include it in your notebook, or copy one of James Whitcomb Riley's poems in your notebook.

Learn the two-letter postal abbreviation of all states in this region.

Make a timeline of Indiana starting in 1679 when René-Robert Cavalier Sieur de la Salle explored it.

Select from the list of state projects on page 121.

POINTS OF INTEREST

Illinois

Mapping

- Draw and label Mississippi River.
- Label Indiana, Kentucky, Missouri, Iowa, and Wisconsin.
- Label Springfield with a star.

- Shade and label Lake Shelbyville.
- Draw and label Kaskaskia, Fox, Sangamon, Rock, and Kankakee rivers.

- Place a brown triangle at Charles Mound and label it with name and elevation.
- Shade and label Carlyle Lake, and Lake Michigan.
- Draw and label Mississippi and Illinois rivers.
- Label Indiana, Kentucky, Missouri, Iowa, and Wisconsin.
- Label Springfield, Chicago, East St. Louis, and Peoria.

Trail Blazing

As a Matter of Fact…

Abraham Lincoln christened the city named after him with watermelon juice and provided watermelon to those in attendance. Add this and any other interesting "Matter of Fact" to your notebook.

Geography Terms
knoll
upstream

The Chicago River is known as the river that flows backward. Read about the engineering feat that reversed the flow of the river and why it was necessary. Write or tell about what you learned.

Illinois has the largest concentration of transportation facilities in the world. Learn how its location helps make it so. Write about what you learned.

Illinois is a principal center of printing and often leads the nation in production of foodstuffs, especially soybeans and corn. Read about the geography, climate, and natural resources. Tell how each of these are related to one another and how they affect the state's economy.

Chicago is home to the world's first skyscraper. Three of the world's five tallest buildings help make Chicago one of the world's most beautiful skylines. List the names of some prominent buildings. Obtain a picture of the Chicago skyline and see how many buildings you can name.

Name some famous people from Illinois and what they accomplished. Choose one person to write about and include it in your notebook.

The Piasa Bird, one of the world's most mysterious prehistoric remains, is painted high on a bluff near Alton. Read about about the Piasa Bird. Include a picture of it in your notebook.

Make a timeline of Illinois starting in 1673 when Marquette and Joliet explored the region.

Select from the list of state projects on page 121.

Geography Through Art
American Cityscape – draw your own skyline.

Week 16

Midwest

GEOGRAPHY TRAILS
Week 17 - Midwestern States

Day 1

The Upper Peninsula of Michigan is connected to what state? The capital of Minnesota lies along what river?

What national park is located on the northern border of Minnesota? Over half of the population of Minnesota lives in or near the twin cities; what two cities make up the twin cities?

What are the chief products of Wisconsin? Does Wisconsin have a higher or lower population of American Indians than Minnesota?

Day 2

What Great Lake forms a coastline along the shores of Minnesota, Wisconsin, and Michigan? Is the northernmost part of Minnesota farther north than Maine? (Be careful!)

What four states surround the state of Wisconsin? The Mississippi River begins at what source?

How high is Wisconsin's cascade waterfall, Big Manitou, and in what city is it located? What are the longitude and latitude coordinates of Green Bay, WI?

Day 3

What lakes form part of Wisconsin's boundary? What two rivers form Wisconsin's eastern boundary?

What two rivers form the boundary between Minnesota and Wisconsin? Is Minnesota's land area near Lake of the Woods, north or south of Maine's northernmost border?

What is the name of Minnesota's famous waterfall, and what is its height? What city in Minnesota has the highest population and is ranked among the 50 largest U.S. cities?

Day 4

What is the two-letter postal abbreviation for Minnesota? What is the state nickname for Wisconsin?

Where is Green Bay located? What is the largest of Wisconsin's nearly 15,000 lakes?

What is the source of the Minnesota River and where does it empty? What percentage of the land area of Minnesota is forested? (See formula hint on student reference sheet page 121.)

POINTS OF INTEREST

Wisconsin

Mapping

- Draw and label Mississippi River.
- Shade and label Lake Superior and Lake Michigan.
- Label Michigan, Minnesota, Iowa, and Illinois.
- Label Madison with a star.

- Shade and label Petenwell Lake.
- Draw and label St. Croix and Chippewa rivers.
- Label Green Bay and Door Peninsula.

- Place a brown triangle at Timms Hill and label its name and elevation.
- Shade and label Lake Superior, Lake Michigan, and Lake Winnebago.
- Draw and label Black, Wisconsin, and Mississippi rivers.
- Label Michigan, Minnesota, Iowa, and Illinois.
- Label Madison, Green Bay, Milwaukee, and Wisconsin Dells.

Trail Blazing

As a Matter of Fact...

So many of Green Bay's paper mills make bathroom tissue that it is known as the Toilet Paper Capital of the World. (And you thought Wisconsin only made cheese!) Add this and any other interesting "Matter of Fact" to your notebook.

Read about Wisconsin's name, state symbols, and motto. Tell what you learned.

> **Geography Terms**
> downstream
> pond

Learn how Wisconsin's culture has been influenced by early settlers from Germany and Scandinavia. Tell or write about what you learned.

Wisconsin's 1.6 million dairy cows produce enough milk to supply 42 million people a year with milk; in addition, they supply one fourth of the nation's butter and almost half of its cheese. Learn about dairy farming or list the steps for making cheese.

In 1884 the first Ringling Brothers Circus played to a crowd of 52 near their hometown of Baraboo. Obtain a tourist brochure from Circus World Museum in Baraboo to learn the history of American circuses. (550 Water Street, Baraboo, WI 53913, 1-866-693-1500)

Name some famous people from Wisconsin and what they accomplished. Choose one person to write about and include it in your notebook, or put pictures of some of Frank Lloyd Wright's buildings in your notebook.

Review the states and capitals of this region by using flash cards, making a crossword puzzle, or playing Concentration.

Make a timeline of Wisconsin starting in 1634 when Jean Nicolet landed on Green Bay shore.

Select from the list of state projects on page 121.

POINTS OF INTEREST

Minnesota

Mapping

- Shade and label Lake Superior.
- Draw and label Mississippi River.
- Label Wisconsin, Iowa, South Dakota, North Dakota, and Canada.
- Label St. Paul with a star.

- Shade and label Mesabi Range.
- Shade and label Leech Lake, Mills Lacs, and Vermilion Lake.

- Place a brown triangle at Eagle Mountain and label its name and elevation.
- Shade and label Lake Superior, Upper Red Lake, Lower Red Lake, and Lake of the Woods.
- Draw and label Minnesota, Mississippi, St. Croix, Red, and Rainy rivers.
- Label Wisconsin, Iowa, South Dakota, North Dakota, and Canada.
- Label St. Paul, Minneapolis, International Falls, and Bloomington.

Trail Blazing

As a Matter of Fact…

The Mall of America in Bloomington, the largest shopping mall in the United States, has about 400 stores, an amusement park, and an aquarium! Add this and any other interesting "Matter of Fact" to your notebook.

Read about Minnesota's name, state symbols, and motto. Tell what you learned.

Minnesota sits on three continental watersheds. Learn about watersheds. List these three water-sheds and where they flow.

The source of the great Mississippi River is at Lake Itasca, where it is only about ten feet wide and two feet deep. List all the states through which the Mississippi passes.

Minnesota produces more butter than any other state. Read about the geography, climate, and natural resources. Tell how each of these are related to one another and how they affect the state's economy.

Name some famous people from Minnesota and what they accomplished. Choose one person to write about and include it in your notebook, or copy one of Garrison Keillor's stories or poems in your notebook.

Charles Mayo, who helped establish the world-famous Mayo Clinic in Rochester, began his career at age nine, administering ether to patients for operations. Study the Mayo clinic and its accomplishments. Identify what makes it exceptional. Write or tell what you learned.

Make a timeline of Minnesota starting in 1679 when Daniel Greysolon, Sieru Duluth, explored it.

Select from the list of state projects on page 121.

GEOGRAPHY TRAILS
Week 18 - Midwestern States

Day 1

How many states share a boundary with Missouri? What river flows through the middle of Missouri?

How are the northern and southern regions of Missouri different? What is the name of the plateau south of the Missouri River?

Iowa is the top producer of what grain? Which state has the most number of farms: Indiana, Illinois, or Iowa?

Day 2

What state is north of Missouri? What river flows through Iowa's state capital?

Do more rivers in Iowa flow toward the Mississippi River or toward the Missouri River? If you were heading south from Des Moines, IA, in what direction would you need to turn to get to Lake Red Rock?

Is the highest point in Iowa higher or lower than the highest point in Missouri? Is the elevation of Des Moines, IA, higher or lower than Duluth, MN?

Day 3

What two rivers make up Iowa's eastern and western boundaries? What is the capital of Iowa?

Ninety percent of the land in Iowa is farmland; how do the many rivers in this state contribute to the land use? What is Iowa's state nickname?

Is the average annual precipitation of Des Moines, IA, higher or lower than that of Kansas City, MO? Does Missouri or Iowa consume more BTUs of energy?

Day 4

What mountains are in the southern part of Missouri? In what city is the Gateway Arch located?

Is Kansas City in Missouri or Kansas? What river, south of Missouri's capital, flows through the Lake of the Ozarks?

Is the average acreage per farm in Missouri higher or lower than in Iowa? What is the climate of Missouri?

POINTS OF INTEREST

Iowa

Mapping

- Draw and label Des Moines and Mississippi rivers.
- Label Minnesota, Wisconsin, Illinois, Missouri, Nebraska, and South Dakota.
- Label Des Moines with a star.

- Place a brown triangle at the highest point and label the elevation.
- Draw and label Des Moines, Cedar, Big Sioux, Missouri, and Mississippi rivers.
- Label Minnesota, Wisconsin, Illinois, Missouri, Nebraska, and South Dakota.
- Label Des Moines, Cedar Rapids, Davenport, and Sioux City.

Trail Blazing

As a Matter of Fact...

Iowa's first "road" was actually a furrow plowed from Dubuque to Iowa City. It is believed to be the longest furrow ever plowed. Add this and any other interesting "Matter of Fact" to your notebook.

> **Geography Terms**
> cavern
> field

Read about Iowa's name, state symbols, and motto. Tell what you learned.

Iowa is the third largest agricultural state. Find out what goods are produced there. Read about the geography, climate, and natural resources. Tell how each of these are related to one another and how they affect the state's economy.

Learn about the Amana Colonies, their influence, their way of life. Explore how they have contributed to the culture of the state.

Read about the Iowa Caucus, and what role it plays in presidential campaigns. Write a short summary and place in your notebook.

Make a crossword puzzle with Midwestern states as clues and their capitals as answers.

Name some famous people from Iowa and what they accomplished. Choose one person to write about and include it in your notebook.

Learn the postal abbreviations for all the states in this region.

Make a timeline of Iowa starting in 1673 when Marquette and Joliet first claimed the land for France.

Select from the list of state projects on page 121.

POINTS OF INTEREST

Missouri

Mapping

- Draw and label Missouri River.
- Label Iowa, Illinois, Kentucky, Tennessee, Arkansas, Oklahoma, Kansas, and Nebraska.
- Label Jefferson City with a star.

- Shade and label the Ozark Plateau.
- Draw and label Osage and St. Francis rivers.
- Label Springfield and Cape Girardeau.

- Place a brown triangle at Taum Sauk Mountain and label its name and elevation.
- Shade and label the Lake of the Ozarks and Table Rock Lakes.
- Draw and label Missouri and Mississippi rivers.
- Label Iowa, Illinois, Kentucky, Tennessee, Arkansas, Oklahoma, Kansas, and Nebraska.
- Label Jefferson City, Kansas City, and St. Louis.

Trail Blazing

As a Matter of Fact...

St. Louis was founded by 14-year-old René Auguste Chouteau in 1764. Add this and any other interesting "Matter of Fact" to your notebook.

> **Geography Terms**
> hill
> cape

St. Louis, considered the "Gateway to the West," has the tallest monument in the U.S., the Gateway Arch. Obtain a tourist brochure to learn how it was constructed and about its unique elevator system that takes tourists to the top.

Missouri has some of the biggest underground springs in the world. Big Spring, the largest in the U.S., pumps over eleven million gallons of water daily into the Current River. Study the formation of springs and mark locations of springs on your Missouri map.

The Pony Express began its mail delivery in Missouri in 1860. Mail could be carried on horseback 2000 miles from St. Joseph, MO, to San Francisco, CA, in ten days. Study the history of the Pony Express. Write a report; include a map of the route and tell why it ended abruptly.

Missouri is the center of U.S. barite mining. Learn the uses for barite and how it's mined, or read about the geography, climate, and natural resources. Tell how each of these are related to one another and how they affect the state's economy.

Name some famous people from Missouri and what they accomplished. Choose one person to write about and include it in your notebook, or make a list of books by Mark Twain.

Make a timeline of Missouri starting in 1762 when René-Robert Cavelier, Sieur de La Salle, claimed Missouri for France.

Select from the list of state projects on page 121.

Geography Through Art
Chain Saw Art – carving soap

GEOGRAPHY TRAILS
Week 19 - Midwestern States

Day 1

🐾 What river flows through South Dakota's capital city? What state is east of South Dakota?

🐾 What is the highest point in South Dakota, and where is it located? What two lakes form part of the northeastern boundary of South Dakota?

🐾 How long is the James River in North and South Dakota, and where does it originate? What happened at Wounded Knee, South Dakota, on December 29, 1890?

Day 2

🐾 What lake is south of North Dakota's capital city? Are the Great Plains located in the eastern part of North Dakota or the western part?

🐾 What grain is grown in abundance in North Dakota? What river flows through Minot, ND?

🐾 What are the elevation and north latitude of Sioux Falls, SD? What is the lowest point in Roberts County, SD, and what is the elevation?

Day 3

🐾 In what state is the Black Hills? What river flows from Canada to form the boundary between North Dakota and Minnesota?

🐾 In what part of North Dakota are the Badlands? What is the highest point in North Dakota, and where is it located?

🐾 Which state produces more crude oil: North Dakota, or South Dakota? Which state has no hazardous waste sites: North Dakota or South Dakota?

Day 4

🐾 What is South Dakota's state bird? In what state is Mount Rushmore located?

🐾 Where are the Black Hills of South Dakota? What famous national memorial is carved in granite in the Black Hills?

🐾 Is North Dakota ranked in the top five states for per capita energy consumption? Describe the climate of South Dakota.

POINTS OF INTEREST

North Dakota

Mapping

- Draw and label Missouri River.
- Label Minnesota, South Dakota, Montana, and Canada.
- Label Bismarck with a star.

- Shade and label the Great Plains yellow and the Badlands orange.

- Place a brown triangle at White Butte and label its name and elevation.
- Shade and label Lake Sakakawea, Lake Oahe, and Devil's Lake.
- Draw and label Missouri, Red, Souris, and James rivers.
- Label Bismarck, Fargo, Jamestown, and Grand Forks.

Trail Blazing

As a Matter of Fact…

Kodak film was so named by its inventor, D. H. Houston, by using a variation of the name Dakota. Add this and any other interesting "Matter of Fact" to your notebook.

Read about North Dakota's name, state symbols, and motto. Tell what you learned.

The first true picture of this vast region came from reports of the Lewis and Clark expedition in 1804. Their exploration of the land and relationships with the Indian tribes helped pave the way for the settlement of the land. Learn more about the Lewis and Clark expedition and write a summary for your notebook.

> **Geography Terms**
> valley
> cliff

North Dakota leads the nation in the number of coal reserves. Make a list of the uses for coal.

Read about the geography, climate, and natural resources. Tell how each of these are related to one another and how they affect the state's economy.

The International Peace Garden is located in both North Dakota and Canada. Learn what it is about and tell what you learned.

An average North Dakota farmer grows enough food to feed 129 people a year. Learn what products they grow and where this state ranks in wheat production. Consider the relationship between the state's location, its weather, and its agricultural industry.

Name some famous people from North Dakota and what they accomplished. Choose one person to write about and include it in your notebook.

Make a timeline of North Dakota starting in 1738 when Pierre Gaultier de Varennes, Sieur de La Vérendrye, explored there.

Select from the list of state projects on page 121.

POINTS OF INTEREST

South Dakota

Mapping

- Draw and label Missouri River.
- Label North Dakota, Minnesota, Iowa, Nebraska, Wyoming, and Montana.
- Label Pierre with a star.

- Shade and label the Great Plains yellow and the Black Hills gray.
- Shade and label Lake Francis Case and Lewis and Clark Lake.

- Place a brown triangle at Harney Peak and label its name and elevation.
- Shade and label Lake Oahe.
- Draw and label Missouri, Cheyenne, Bell Fourche, White, and Big Sioux rivers.
- Label North Dakota, Minnesota, Iowa, Nebraska, Wyoming, and Montana.
- Label Pierre, Rapid City, Sioux Falls, and Lead.

Trail Blazing

As a Matter of Fact...

President Benjamin Harrison never revealed which statehood bill he signed first the day both North Dakota and South Dakota became official states. They have been listed as 39th and 40th by alphabetical order. Add this and any other interesting "Matter of Fact" to your notebook.

Read about South Dakota's name, state symbols, and motto. Tell what you learned.

Learn about the typical daily life of the Sioux Indian Tribe and about their leader Sitting Bull.

South Dakota is the nation's leading producer of gold. Its Homestake Mine holds the world record for total production of a single gold mine. Learn what type of soil or geological features gold is found.

South Dakota's main industries are agriculture and tourism. Read about the geography, climate, and natural resources. Tell how each of these are related to one another and how they affect the state's economy.

Learn how Mount Rushmore was carved out of the granite mountainside. How many men were involved, what tools did they use, and how long did it take?

Name some famous people from South Dakota and what they accomplished. Choose one person to write about and include it in your notebook.

Make a timeline of South Dakota starting in 1682 when René-Robert Cavelier Sieur de La Salle claimed the land for France.

Select from the list of state projects on page 121.

Geography Through Art

Mount Rushmore – draw your own model.

GEOGRAPHY TRAILS

Week 20 - Midwestern States

Day 1

🐾 What is the state tree of Nebraska? What river in Nebraska branches north into Wyoming and south into Colorado?

🐾 What is the highest point in Kansas, and where is it located? What is the land area of Kansas, and what is its rank?

🐾 Cherry County is the largest county in Nebraska; what is the next largest county and how many square miles difference are there between the two? (hint: states, U.S., counties) In what city is the county seat of the highest populated county in Nebraska?

Day 2

🐾 What is the state nickname of South Dakota? What is the capital of Nebraska?

🐾 What is the state nickname for Kansas? Why did settlers in Kansas build their homes with sod?

🐾 What percentage Nebraska's land area is farmland? (See formula hint on student reference sheet page 121.) What chief crops are grown in Nebraska?

Day 3

🐾 What is the two-letter postal abbreviation for Kansas? What river flows through the capital city of Kansas?

🐾 Is most of Nebraska land used for farming, industry, or mining? On what river is Lake McConaughy in Nebraska?

🐾 Does Kansas produce any crude oil? List the 12 midwestern states in order from highest to lowest by their corn crop.

Day 4

🐾 What state is east of Kansas? What river flows through the famous wild west town of Dodge City?

🐾 What state is southwest of Nebraska? What Nebraska lake is named after famous explorers?

🐾 What kinds of trees are used to produce lumber in Kansas? What is the highest temperature recorded in Kansas, and when did it occur?

POINTS OF INTEREST

Nebraska

Mapping

- Draw and label Missouri River.
- Label South Dakota, Iowa, Missouri, Kansas, Colorado, and Wyoming.
- Label Lincoln with a star.

- Shade and label the Great Plains yellow and the Sand Hills pink.
- Draw and label Elkhorn and Niobrara rivers.
- Using a fresh map of the United States, shade and label the Great Plains and the Rocky Mountains.

- Place a brown triangle at the highest point in Kimball County and label the elevation.
- Shade and label Lewis and Clark Lake and Lake McConaughy.
- Draw and label North Platte, South Platte, and Missouri rivers.
- Label South Dakota, Iowa, Missouri, Kansas, Colorado, and Wyoming.
- Label Lincoln, North Platte, Omaha, Scottsbluff, and Norfolk.

Trail Blazing

As a Matter of Fact…

Nebraska currently has the only state government with a unicameral (one house) legislature; it has a Senate only. Add this and any other interesting "Matter of Fact" to your notebook.

> **Geography Terms** review

Read about Nebraska's name, state symbols, and motto. Tell what you learned.

Nebraska is one of 16 states that chose the honeybee as its state insect. Make a list of the other 15. (hint: http://www.netstate.com/states/tables/state_insects.htm)

The Nebraska Sand Hills, covering 20,000 square miles of sand dune fields, are the largest sand sea in the western hemisphere. Describe what conditions are needed for sand dunes to form.

The nation's first land claim from the Homestead Act of 1862 was made in Nebraska. Study this act and its impact on the settlement of the Great Plains states. Learn why many settlers built their homes of sod, and describe the process.

Nearly 95% of the land area of Nebraska is used for farming and grazing. Study how the soil and weather conditions in this Great Plains state affect the economy. Write a report and include information on the Ogallala Aquifer.

Name some famous people from Nebraska and what they accomplished. Choose one person to write about and include it in your notebook.

Make a timeline of Nebraska starting in 1793 when Pierre and Paul Mallet explored it.

Select from the list of state projects on page 121.

POINTS OF INTEREST

Kansas

Mapping

- Draw and label Arkansas River.
- Label Nebraska, Missouri, Oklahoma, and Colorado.
- Label Topeka with a star.

- Shade and label Milford Reservoir.

- Place a brown triangle at Mount Sunflower and label its name and elevation.
- Draw and label Republican, Arkansas, Saline, Smoky Hill, Kansas and Missouri Rivers.
- Label Topeka, Kansas City, Wichita, and Dodge City.

Trail Blazing

As a Matter of Fact...

Dodge City bankers and businessmen once accepted dry buffalo bones as legal tender. Add this and any other interesting "Matter of Fact" to your notebook.

Read about Kansas's name, state symbols, and motto. Tell what you learned.

The geographic center of the conterminous states is located in Smith County, Kansas, near Lebanon. Learn what "geographic center" means and define "conterminous."

Thanks to Russian immigrants who brought with them Red Winter Wheat seeds in the 1800s, Kansas has become the nation's leading wheat producer. Read about wheat production and describe what kind of climate wheat needs to grow.

Learn what industries contribute to the economy of Kansas. Read about the geography, climate, and natural resources. Tell how each of these are related to one another and how they affect the state's economy.

Three hundred years ago, 70 million buffalo, or bison, roamed the Kansas plains. Study the history of buffalo, their uses to Native Americans, and efforts at preventing their extinction. Include a summary in your notebook.

The U.S. has more tornadoes than any other country in the world. Kansas sits in a region called Tornado Alley. Study tornadoes and what weather conditions cause them.

Name some famous people from Kansas and what they accomplished. Choose one person to write about and include it in your notebook, or include a picture of Amelia Earhart in your notebook.

Make a timeline of Kansas starting in 1541 when Francisco Vásquez de Coronado explored its land.

Select from the list of state projects on page 121.

GEOGRAPHY TRAILS
Week 21 - Review

Day 1

What is the capital of Minnesota? Are most of Minnesota's over 10,000 lakes located in the northern part or southern part of the state?

On what Michigan island would you more likely travel by bike or on foot? If you drove 200 miles southwest from the capital of Iowa, in what capital city would you arrive?

Which two Midwest states have the highest percentage of public high school graduation rates? What was the lowest temperature recorded for Wisconsin, and when did it occur?

Day 2

What is the postal abbreviation for Iowa? What is the state flower of Kansas?

What capital cities are located along the Missouri River? Is Badlands, National Park located east or west of the Missouri River?

What are names and locations of the tallest building and the tallest structure in the U.S.? What are the longitude and latitude coordinates of Akron, OH?

Day 3

Are the Great Plains located in the eastern or western part of Nebraska? What is the capital of Wisconsin?

Does Military Ridge lie north or south of the Wisconsin River? In what state is the Ozark Plateau?

Which midwestern state has the lowest violent crime rate? What two midwestern states are among the top ten crude oil producers in the U.S.?

Day 4

What state shares North Dakota's western boundary? What is the postal abbreviation for Nebraska?

What is Minnesota's state nickname? List the following states in order by area from largest to smallest: North Dakota, Minnesota, Missouri, and Kansas.

What three midwestern states rank among the top ten states for total consumption of energy? Which states produce more than 250 million bushels of soybeans annually?

POINTS OF INTEREST

Review

No new assignments.

Use this week to complete any unfinished projects. Make sure you know the following from memory of all states you have studied up to now:

- state capitals
- postal abbreviations
- location - be able to identify each state on an outline map of the U.S.

Organize your State Notebook.

SOUTHWESTERN STATES

Oklahoma
Texas
New Mexico
Arizona

GEOGRAPHY TRAILS
Week 22 - Southwestern States

Day 1

Is the western part of Oklahoma mostly plains or mostly mountainous? What river forms the boundary between Oklahoma and Texas?

In what part of Oklahoma would you find the Ouachita Mountains: SW, NW, SE or NE? Put these states in order by land area from largest to smallest: Arizona, Oklahoma, Texas, New Mexico, and Alaska.

Oklahoma ranks second amongst the fifty states for its population of Native Americans; what state is first? What is the normal high temperature in Oklahoma City in July?

Day 2

What large body of water forms the curved coastline of Texas? What forms the boundary between Texas and Mexico?

Name three lakes south and east of Oklahoma's capital city. What is the state nickname of Oklahoma?

What is the zip code of Tulsa, Oklahoma? (hint: cities, U.S., zip code) What kind of topography describes the western part of Oklahoma?

Day 3

Through what state does the Rio Grande River flow before it reaches Texas? What mountains run through the center of New Mexico?

What two national parks are located west of the Pecos River in Texas? Is the Texas border comprised more of land or water?

What state is the top producer of crude oil? How many miles of shoreline and how many miles of coastline are on the gulf coast of Texas?

Day 4

What is the capital of Arizona? Is the Petrified Forest in the eastern or western part of Arizona?

What is the highest point in Texas, and where is it located? Who produces the most oil: Texas or Oklahoma?

Which state has the highest number of farms? What are the top three major crops grown in Texas?

POINTS OF INTEREST

Oklahoma

Mapping

- Draw and label Canadian River.
- Label Kansas, Missouri, Arkansas, Texas, New Mexico and Colorado.
- Label Oklahoma City with a star.

- Shade and label the Ouachita Mountains.
- Shade and label Grand Lake O' the Cherokees.

- Place a brown triangle at Black Mesa and label its name and elevation.
- Shade and label Eufaula Lake, and Lake Texoma.
- Draw and label Canadian, Arkansas, Red, and Washia rivers.
- Label Kansas, Missouri, Arkansas, Texas, New Mexico and Colorado.
- Label Oklahoma City, Tulsa, Ponca City, and Paul's Valley.

Trail Blazing

As a Matter of Fact...

Each of Oklahoma's 55 native Indian tribes has its own language or distinctive dialect, resulting in more languages spoken in Oklahoma than in Europe! Add this and any other interesting "Matter of Fact" to your notebook.

> **Geography Terms**
> plain
> sea port

Read about Oklahoma's name, state symbols, and motto. Tell what you learned.

Tulsa is the "oil capital of the world." Learn what other industries support the economy of Oklahoma. Read about the geography, climate, and natural resources. Tell how each of these are related to one another and how they affect the state's economy.

Oklahoma is so rich with oil that there are even oil wells on the front lawn of the Capitol. Study oil drilling. Write a summary and place it in your notebook.

The Chisholm Trail was used in the 1870s to lead cattle to the Kansas railroad. Read about the cattle drives, and draw the trail on a map. You may need to enlarge a U.S. map focused on the area from Texas to Kansas.

Name some famous people from Oklahoma and what they accomplished. Choose one person to write about and include it in your notebook.

Learn the two-letter postal abbreviation of all states in this region.

Make a timeline of Oklahoma starting in 1541 when Vásquez de Coronado explored it.

Select from the list of state projects on page 121.

Geography Through Art
Indian Signs and Symbols

POINTS OF INTEREST

Texas

Mapping

- Draw and label Rio Grande.
- Label Louisiana, Arkansas, Oklahoma, New Mexico, Mexico, and Gulf of Mexico.
- Label Austin with a star.

- Shade and label the Edwards Plateau purple and the Great Plains yellow.
- Label Padre Island.

- Place a brown triangle at Guadalupe Peak and label its name and elevation.
- Draw and label Canadian, Colorado, Pecos, and Rio Grande.
- Label Louisiana, Arkansas, Oklahoma, New Mexico, Mexico, and Gulf of Mexico.
- Label Austin, Dallas, Houston, El Paso, Galveston, and Amarillo.

Trail Blazing

As a Matter of Fact...

Texas still retains the right to divide itself into five states, if the people want to do so – a right granted at statehood. Add this and any other interesting "Matter of Fact" to your notebook.

Padre Island is one of the last undeveloped barrier islands in the world. Learn how barrier islands are formed, what role they play in the geography of Texas, and why this one is still undeveloped.

About 20% of Texans are Mexican. Learn about the Tex-Mex history and the people. In what areas do you see influence (food, clothes, etc.)? Prepare a Tex-Mex recipe.

> **Geography Terms**
> shore line
> coastline

Learn what industries support the economy of Texas. Explain the different industries by region. List as many goods as you can that Texas leads the nation in producing.

Name some famous people from Texas and what they accomplished. Choose one person to write about and include it in your notebook, or include a list of Scott Joplin songs.

Texas is the only state with five major ports. Make a list of these ports. Find out what products pass in and out of the U.S. through Texas ports. (hint: try this website as a starting point: http://www.texasports.org/)

Texas has the greatest variety of flowers and reptiles of all the states. Include pictures of either in your notebook.

Memorize the states and capitals of this region through making flash cards, playing Concentration, or making a crossword puzzle.

Make a timeline of Texas starting in 1519 when Alonso Alvarez de Pineda landed on the Texas coast.

Select from the list of state projects on page 121.

GEOGRAPHY TRAILS
Week 23 - Southwestern States

Day 1

What is the capital of Oklahoma? What Oklahoma lake is located at the border with Texas?

What four states converge at the point named Four Corners? In what national park would you find the largest natural cave room in the world?

Of all the Native American tribes which two have the highest population? What are Arizona's record high and low temperatures, and when were they recorded?

Day 2

On what river is the capital of Texas located? What is the two-letter postal abbreviation for Texas?

In what part of New Mexico are the San Andreas Mountains? In what part of New Mexico are the Great Plains?

What is the largest gorge in the United States; how long and how deep is it? How many miles long and how many miles wide is Arizona?

Day 3

What is the state bird of New Mexico? New Mexico has the oldest state capital; what is its name?

What large area of land in southwest Arizona has very little moisture or vegetation? In what state is the Grand Canyon National Park?

What is the lowest point in New Mexico, and what is its elevation? During which census did the population of New Mexico exceed 1,000,000 people?

Day 4

What river flows through the Grand Canyon? What state is east of Arizona?

What is the land area of Arizona, and where is it ranked by area? What is the highest point in Arizona and where is it located?

Which of the following southwestern states has the most hazardous waste sites: Arizona, Oklahoma, New Mexico, or Texas? Which of these New Mexico counties has the highest population density: Bernalillo County or Valencia County?

POINTS OF INTEREST

New Mexico

Mapping

- Draw and label Rio Grande.
- Label Oklahoma, Texas, Arizona, Colorado, and Mexico.
- Label Santa Fe with a star.

- Shade and label the Rocky Mountains, the Black Range, San Andreas Mountains, and the Sangre de Cristo Mountains.
- Place x's along the Continental Divide.
- Shade the Colorado Plateau purple and the Great Plains yellow.

- Place a brown triangle at Wheeler Peak and label its name and elevation.
- Draw and label the Pecos River, Rio Grande, and Gila River.
- Label Oklahoma, Texas, Arizona, Colorado,. and Mexico.
- Label Santa Fe, Albuquerque, Las Cruces, Los Alamos, Roswell, and Shiprock.

Trail Blazing

As a Matter of Fact…

Capulin Mountain (at Capulin Volcano National Monument) is one of the few extinct volcanoes in the world that visitors can walk into. Add this and any other interesting "Matter of Fact" to your notebook.

> **Geography Terms**
> desert
> canyon

Read about New Mexico's name, state symbols, and motto. Tell what you learned.

Carlsbad Caverns is one of the world's largest underground caves. Learn about how caves are formed. Include pictures and cave terminology such as stalagmite and stalactite in your notebook.

Read about the geography, climate, and natural resources. Tell how each of these are related to one another and how they affect the state's economy.

New Mexico has many fascinating Pueblo ruins that demonstrate their skill with masonry, weaving, irrigation system, tools, and jewelry. Read about the Pueblos. Write a report for your notebook. Include pictures and drawings.

Los Alamos was the top-secret site where the first atomic bomb was developed. Learn about its fascinating history and what kind of work is done at Los Alamos National Laboratory today.

New Mexico leads the nation in dry ice production from their carbon dioxide wells. Learn how dry ice is produced and how it is used. Make a list of the steps to produce dry ice.

Review states and capitals of this region.

Make a timeline of New Mexico starting in 1598 when Juan de Onate established the first Spanish colony.

Select from the list of state projects on page 121.

POINTS OF INTEREST

Arizona

Mapping

- Draw and label Colorado River.
- Label New Mexico, Utah, Nevada, California, and Mexico.
- Label Phoenix with a star.

- Shade and label the Colorado Plateau purple and the Sonoran Desert orange.

- Place a brown triangle at Humphreys Peak, and label its name and elevation.
- Shade and label Lake Mead.
- Draw and label Gila and Colorado rivers.
- Label Phoenix, Tucson, Prescott, Flagstaff, and Yuma.

Trail Blazing

As a Matter of Fact…

The world's largest solar telescope is at Kitt's Peak National Observatory in Sells. Add this and any other interesting "Matter of Fact" to your notebook.

Read about Arizona's name, state symbols, and motto. Tell what you learned.

The Navajo, the largest Indian tribe, resides in the largest reservation in the U.S. Read about the Navaho nation, and its history and culture. Write a summary in your notebook or tell what you learned.

Arizona has led the nation in copper production since 1907 and leads all states in the value of non-fuel mineral production. Read about the geography, climate, and natural resources. Tell how each of these are related to one another and how they affect the state's economy.

Arizona has numerous natural wonders, including the Grand Canyon, Petrified Forest, Painted Desert, and more. Select one of interest and learn what makes it unique. Put a picture in your notebook along with a description of this wonder and why you chose it.

Arizona's geography and climate are diverse. Snowcapped mountains are only hours away from dry, barren deserts. Study different flora and fauna of Arizona. Learn also of its unique wildlife. List the climate and conditions necessary for each to thrive.

Name some famous people from Arizona and what they accomplished. Choose one person to write about and include it in your notebook.

Learn why Arizona was amongst the last of the states to join the union. Write a summary of what you learned and place it in your notebook.

Make a timeline of Arizona starting in 1200 when the Hopi village of Oraibi was founded.

Select from the list of state projects on page 121.

Geography Through Art
Sand Painting

ROCKY MOUNTAIN STATES

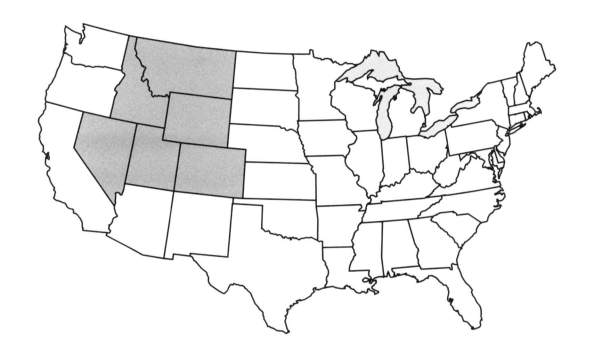

Montana
Idaho
Wyoming
Colorado
Utah
Nevada

GEOGRAPHY TRAILS
Week 24 - Rocky Mountain States

Day 1

Is the western part of Colorado mostly mountainous or mostly plains? What state is north of Colorado?

Colorado has 54 mountain peaks over 14,000 ft; which is the highest, and where is it located? What Colorado national park features ancient Anasazi cliff dwellings?

What percentage of Colorado students who entered 9th grade in 1995 graduated four years later, and how does Colorado's graduation rate rank among the 50 states? (hint: U.S., education) What are the chief nonfuel minerals produced in Colorado?

Day 2

Is Denver, CO located in the mountains? What large lake is located in northern Utah?

Where is the Colorado Plateau located? What winter sport brings tourists from around the world to Colorado?

Is the per capita income of Colorado higher or lower than in Arizona? What percentage of the land area of Colorado is federally owned?

Day 3

What river flows through Arches National Park, Canyonlands National Park, and Lake Powell? What is the two-letter postal abbreviation for Utah?

Where is the Wyoming Basin? What reservoir is located on the North Platte River southwest of Casper, WY?

The world's first national park is located predominately in Wyoming; what is its name, and when was it designated as a national park? What state has the most major coal mines?

Day 4

What state shares Utah's western boundary? What lake is west of Nevada's capital city?

Are Wyoming's Bighorn Mountains near Idaho, Montana, Utah, or Nebraska? In what corner is Wyoming's state capital?

The lowest point in Wyoming is higher than the highest elevation in how many states? What are the chief industries of Wyoming?

POINTS OF INTEREST

Montana

Mapping

- Draw and label Columbia River.
- Label Canada, North Dakota, South Dakota, Wyoming, and Idaho.
- Label Helena with a star.

- Shade and label the Rocky Mountains. Place x's along the Continental Divide.
- Label the Bitterroot Range and Lewis Range, and shade the Great Plains yellow.

- Place a brown triangle at Granite Peak and label its name and elevation.
- Shade and label Fort Peck Lake, Flathead Lake, and Canyon Ferry Lake.
- Draw and label Columbia, Milk, Missouri, and Yellowstone rivers.
- Label Helena, Bozeman, Missoula, and Billings.

Trail Blazing

As a Matter of Fact...

For over 300 years swarms of grasshoppers have been frozen in the ice of the Grasshopper Glacier near Cooke City. Add this and any other interesting "Matter of Fact" to your notebook.

> **Geography Terms**
> basin
> peak

Read about Montana's name, state symbols, and motto. Tell what you learned.

Montana holds the world record for the greatest temperature change in 24 hours. On January 23, 1916 the temperature in Browning plummeted exactly 100 degrees, from 44 degrees above zero to 56 degrees below zero! Learn about the climate in Montana.

Read about the geography, climate, and natural resources. Tell how each of these are related to one another and how they affect the state's economy.

In 1877 Chief Joseph surrendered to U.S. troops at Bear Paw with these final words, "I will fight no more… forever." Read about the Nez Percé nation and their phenomenal 1600-mile retreat.

There are over 50 glaciers in Glacier National Park. Read about the formation of glaciers and how they carve the earth's terrain. Write or tell about what you learned.

Montana is rich with minerals. Learn what these minerals are. Make a list or chart of the minerals and and tell how they are used in industry.

Name some famous people from Montana and what they accomplished. Choose one person to write about and include it in your notebook.

Make a timeline of Montana starting in 1743 when it was explored by Francois and Louis-Joseph la Verendrye.

Select from the list of state projects on page 121.

POINTS OF INTEREST

Idaho

Mapping

- Draw and label Snake River.
- Label Canada, Montana, Wyoming, Utah, Nevada, Oregon, and Washington.
- Label Boise with a star.

- Shade and label the Rocky Mountains, Salmon River Mountains, Wasach Range, and Bitterroot Range.
- Label American Falls Reservoir and Palisades Reservoir.

- Place a brown triangle at Borah Peak and label its name and elevation.
- Shade and label Pend Oreille, Coeur d' Alene, and Bear lakes.
- Draw and label Snake, Clearwater, and Salmon rivers.
- Label Canada, Montana, Wyoming, Utah, Nevada, Oregon, and Washington.
- Label Boise, Idaho Falls, Lewiston, and Pocatello.

Trail Blazing

As a Matter of Fact...

At 33-miles, Island Park claims the longest Main Street in the U.S. Add this and any other interesting "Matter of Fact" to your notebook.

Read about Idaho's name, state symbols, and motto. Tell what you learned.

Idaho produces 72 different types of precious and semiprecious gemstones. Learn how opal, star sapphire, jade, or agate is processed and list its uses in industry.

The state capitol building in Boise is heated with geothermal energy. Read about this process and explain it in your own words.

Idaho produces about two-thirds of the nation's processed potatoes. Read about the geography, climate, and natural resources. Tell how each of these are related to one another and how they affect the state's economy.

More than 80% of all the commercial rainbow trout sold in the U.S. comes from Thousand Springs in the Snake River Valley. Learn how the trout are prepared for shipping. Write about what you learned.

Name some famous people from Idaho and what they accomplished. Choose one person to write about and include it in your notebook.

Begin to memorize the states and capitals of this region through making flash cards, playing Concentration, or making a crossword puzzle.

Make a timeline of Idaho starting in 1805 with Lewis and Clark's expedition.

Select from the list of state projects on page 121.

GEOGRAPHY TRAILS
Week 25 - Rocky Mountain States

Day 1

🐾 What river is west of the Bighorn Mountains in Wyoming? Are the Rocky Mountains located in the eastern or western part of Wyoming?

🐾 The Bitteroot Range forms the rugged boundary between what two states? Is Montana's capital city in the mountains or in the plains?

🐾 Which of the Rocky Mountain states has the lowest burglary rate? Is the average wind speed in Helena, MT more or less than the average wind speed in Casper, WY?

Day 2

🐾 What is the capital of Wyoming? What river flows across the southern part of Idaho?

🐾 What is Montana's state nickname? What is the highest point in Montana, and where is it located?

🐾 What are the north latitude and west longitude of Great Falls, MT and what is its elevation? The land area of Montana is at least four times the size of how many U.S. states?

Day 3

🐾 What lake is located in the northern panhandle of Idaho? What two rivers cross the border of Montana and North Dakota?

🐾 What mountain range, in southeast Idaho, lies between Bear Lake and Blackfoot Reservoir? Along what Idaho river is the American Falls Reservoir?

🐾 Idaho is home to the deepest canyon in North America. What is its name and how deep is it? What percentage* of U.S.-grown potatoes is produced in Idaho? * See formula hint on page 121.

Day 4

🐾 What is the capital of Montana? What is the state tree of Montana?

🐾 Where are the Salmon River Mountains? If you phoned a friend in Lexington, KY, from your ski vacation in Sun Valley, ID, what time would you need to call to reach him at 7:30 A.M. during breakfast?

🐾 Is the highest recorded temperature in Idaho higher or lower than that of highest in Texas? What is the difference in feet between Idaho's highest point and it lowest point?

POINTS OF INTEREST

Wyoming

Mapping

- Draw and label Bighorn River.
- Label Montana, South Dakota, Nebraska, Colorado, Utah, and Idaho.
- Label Cheyenne with a star.

- Shade and label the Rocky Mountains, Bighorn Mountains, and Laramie Mountains.
- Shade the Great Plains yellow.
- Shade and label Yellowstone Lake, Boysen Reservoir, Flaming Gorge Reservoir, and Pathfinder Reservoir.

- Place a brown triangle at Gannett Peak and label its name and elevation.
- Draw and label North Platte, Bighorn, and Green rivers.
- Label Montana, South Dakota, Nebraska, Colorado, Utah, and Idaho.
- Label Cheyenne, Jackson, Casper, and Gillette.

Trail Blazing

As a Matter of Fact...

When telephone poles were first placed in Wyoming, as many as 30 buffalo could be seen waiting their turn to use one as a scratching post. Add this and any other interesting "Matter of Fact" to your notebook.

> **Geography Terms**
> gorge
> precipice

Read about Wyoming's name, state symbols, and motto. Tell what you learned.

More than 80% of Wyoming's land is used for cattle grazing. Read about the geography, climate, and natural resources. Tell how each of these are related to one another and how they affect the state's economy.

Wyoming ranks last in population of all states at five people per square mile. Using an outline map of the U.S., shade the states according to population density. Use your student atlas for the data.

Yellowstone National Park is known for its geysers. Learn how geysers are formed. Tell or write about what you learned. Include a picture of Old Faithful or any other geyser in your notebook.

Grand Teton National Park is known for the interesting rock formations. Make a travel brochure depicting that park's natural features.

At only 15 years old, Buffalo Bill Cody rode 322 miles in Wyoming for the Pony Express (a Pony Express record!) when he discovered his replacement had been killed. Read about the life of this colorful character of western history and write a human interest newspaper article about what you learned.

Name some famous people from Wyoming and what they accomplished. Choose one person to write about and include it in your notebook.

Make a timeline of Wyoming starting in 1743 when Francois and Louis La Verendrye explored it.

Select from the list of state projects on page 121.

POINTS OF INTEREST

Colorado

Mapping

- Draw and label Arkansas River.
- Label Wyoming, Nebraska, Kansas, Oklahoma, New Mexico, and Utah.
- Label Denver with a star.

- Shade and label the Rocky Mountains, San Juan Mountains, and Sangre de Cristo Mountains.
- Place x's along the Continental Divide.
- Shade the Colorado Plateau purple and the Great Plains yellow.

- Place a brown triangle at Mount Elbert and label its name and elevation.
- Draw and label Arkansas, Rio Grande, Colorado, South Platte, Republican, and Yampa rivers.
- Label Wyoming, Nebraska, Kansas, Oklahoma, New Mexico, and Utah.
- Label Denver, Colorado Springs, Pueblo, Grand Junction, Fort Collins, Aspen, and Durango.

Trail Blazing

As a Matter of Fact...

Colorado's elevation is so high that its Rocky Mountains boast 54 peaks over 14,000 feet tall. In fact, the lowest point in Colorado is higher than the highest point in 18 states. Add this and any other interesting "Matter of Fact" to your notebook.

Learn the history of Colorado's name, state symbols, and motto. Tell about what you learned.

The Royal Gorge Bridge, suspended over the Arkansas River, is the world's highest suspension bridge over water. Read about the construction of suspension bridges. Tell or write about what you learned.

Colorado is a major agricultural, mining, and tourism state. Read about the geography, climate, and natural resources. Tell how each of these are related to one another and how they affect the state's economy.

Colorado Springs is home to the state's defense and aerospace industry. Learn about the Air Force Academy, or find out about the North American Aerospace Defense Command (NORAD) inside hollowed-out Cheyenne Mountain. Write a newspaper article about what you learned.

Read about the Mesa Verde cliff dwellings built by the Anasazi before 1300 A.D. Make a travel brochure telling about what you learned.

Learn what causes the chinook winds in the Rocky Mountains. Write a weather report about it.

Learn the two-letter postal abbreviation of all states in this region.

Make a timeline of Colorado starting in 1540 when Francisco Vásquez de Coronado explored it.

Select from the list of state projects on page 121.

Geography Through Art
Pottery

GEOGRAPHY TRAILS
Week 26 - Rocky Mountain States

Day 1
- What is the two-letter postal abbreviation for Colorado? What is the capital of Utah?
- What is the state nickname of Utah? What part of Utah is desert?
- What is the longest vehicle tunnel in Utah, and how long is it? What percentage of the land area of Utah is federally owned?

Day 2
- What lake forms part of the boundary between Nevada and Arizona? What is the capital of Idaho?
- What is the highest point in Utah, and where is it located? What is unusual about Utah's largest lake?
- What is the lowest point in Utah, and what is its elevation? Through what states does the Continental Divide pass?

Day 3
- Do the Great Plains span Montana's eastern or western land? In what state is the larger part of Yellowstone National Park located?
- What is the area of Nevada, and what is its rank? Do Nevada's Shoshone Mountains run north and south or east and west?
- What are the principal minerals that make Nevada a leading mineral producer? How does the air quality of Las Vegas NV, compare to that of Phoenix, AZ?

Day 4
- What is Utah's state tree? What river flows through Colorado's capital city?
- What national park is located in Nevada near the Utah border? What lake lies on the California-Nevada border and is located over 6,000 feet above sea level?
- What are the chief industries of Nevada? What is the average annual precipitation in Reno, NV, and what is the general climate of the state?

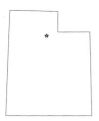

POINTS OF INTEREST

Utah

Mapping

- Draw and label Colorado River.
- Label Idaho, Wyoming, Colorado, Arizona, and Nevada.
- Label Salt Lake City with a star.

- Shade and label the Rocky Mountains and the Uinta Mountains.
- Label Glen Canyon.
- Shade and label the Great Salt Lake Desert orange and the Colorado Plateau purple.

- Place a brown triangle at King's Peak and label its name and elevation.
- Shade and label the Great Salt Lake, Utah Lake, and Lake Powell.
- Draw and label Green, Sevier, Colorado, and San Juan rivers.
- Label Idaho, Wyoming, Colorado, Arizona, and Nevada.
- Label Salt Lake City, Ogden, Provo, and Cedar City.

Trail Blazing

As a Matter of Fact...

Zion Narrows canyon is so deep and narrow, stars are actually visible from the canyon bottom even at the brightest time of day. Add this and any other interesting "Matter of Fact" to your notebook.

> **Geography Terms**
> tunnel
> summit

Read about Utah's name, state symbols, and motto. Tell what you learned.

Utah has a diverse economy, from tourism and manufacturing to mining and agriculture. Find out how such a barren land became so productive. Write or tell what you learned.

The meeting of the Central Pacific Railroad and the Union Pacific Railroad occurred at Promontory in 1869. Read about the construction of the transcontinental railroad and how its completion changed American culture. Tell or write about what you learned.

Utah has a number of interesting rock formations in the southern part of the state. Choose a national park, and make a travel brochure depicting that park's natural features.

Name some famous people from Utah and what they accomplished. Choose one person to write about and include it in your notebook.

Read about the way of life and traditions of the Navajo Nation. Write about what you learned. Include pictures or drawings in your report.

Use flash cards, play Concentration, or make and use a crossword puzzle to review the states and capitals of this region.

Make a timeline of Utah starting in 1776 when Silvestre Velez de Escalante and Francisco Atanasio Dominguez explored it.

Select from the list of state projects on page 121.

POINTS OF INTEREST

Nevada

Mapping

- Draw and label Humboldt River.
- Label Oregon, Idaho, Utah, Arizona, and California.
- Label Carson City with a star.

- Shade and label Shoshone Mountains and Monitor Range.
- Shade and label the Great Basin.

- Place a brown triangle at Boundary Peak and label its name and elevation.
- Shade and label Lake Mead, Lake Tahoe, and Pyramid Lake.
- Draw and label Humboldt and Colorado rivers.
- Label Carson City, Las Vegas, and Reno.

Trail Blazing

As a Matter of Fact...

The entire Nevada constitution was sent to Washington by telegram, to the tune of $3400, in order to meet the deadline of statehood. Add this and any other interesting "Matter of Fact" to your notebook.

Read about Nevada's name, state symbols, and motto. Tell what you learned.

Tourism contributes more to Nevada's economy than agriculture, manufacturing, and mining combined. Read about the geography, climate, and natural resources. Tell how each of these are related to one another and how they affect the state's economy.

The Hoover Dam is the highest concrete arch dam in the nation and generates electricity for Arizona, California, and Nevada. Learn about the dam's construction in the 1930s, why it was needed, and how Lake Mead, the world's largest artificial lake, was also formed at that time.

Nevada is the nation's fastest growing state. Find out why. Make a brochure about Nevada and place it in your notebook.

Find out why Route 375 has been nicknamed Extraterrestrial Highway. Tell what you learned and give your opinion about what people believe about this area.

Name some famous people from Nevada and what they accomplished. Choose one person to write about and include it in your notebook.

Learn about the rare Devil's Hole pupfish found only in Devil's Hole or cui-ui, found only in Pyramid Lake. Write a newspaper article about what you learned.

Make a timeline of Nevada starting in 1821 when it became part of Mexico.

Select from the list of state projects on page 121.

GEOGRAPHY TRAILS
Week - 27 Review

Day 1

What river flows through Arizona's capital city? What is Texas's state bird?

If you traveled 400 miles due west from Wyoming's capital city, at what large body of water would you arrive? In what state is Glacier National Park located?

What president holds the record for the most congressional bills vetoed? Who is the only Speaker of the House from the state of Washington?

Day 2

What is the highest point in Oklahoma? Are the Great Plains or the Colorado Plateau located in the eastern part of New Mexico?

Hoover Dam provides electricity for what three states? The flat land on either side of what river is home to 70% of the population of Idaho?

Who are the two Secretaries of the Interior from Colorado in the past 50 years? What is the highest U.S. dam, and where is it located?

Day 3

What four states make up the Four Corners, where four states meet at one point?

In what national park would you find a geyser named Old Faithful? Gila monsters and ridge-nosed rattlesnakes are at home in what state?

What is the largest U.S. reservoir, and where is it located? What is the longest land vehicular tunnel in the U.S., and how long is it?

Day 4

What is the postal abbreviation for Montana? What two states are located at the southern border of Idaho?

What state produces more oil and natural gas than any other state? What state was called Indian Territory by the government before it became a state in 1907?

In what state would you find floating pontoon drawbridges? Is the Golden Gate Bridge in San Francisco the longest suspension bridge in the U.S.?

POINTS OF INTEREST

Review

No new assignments.

Use this week to complete any unfinished projects. Make sure you know the following from memory of all states you have studied up to now:

- state capitals
- postal abbreviations
- location - be able to identify each state on an outline map of the U.S.

Organize your State Notebook.

PACIFIC COAST STATES

Washington
Oregon
California
Alaska
Hawaii

GEOGRAPHY TRAILS
Week 28 - Pacific Coast States

Day 1

🐾 What mountain range spans the western part of Washington? What river forms part of the southern boundary of Washington?

🐾 What is the name of the mountain in Washington's Cascade Mountains that erupted in 1980? What passageway of water connects the Pacific Ocean to Puget Sound?

🐾 What is the county seat of the most populated county in Washington? Three of the ten largest national champion trees are located in Washington; where are the trees located and what kinds of trees are they?

Day 2

🐾 What is the capital of Washington? What river forms a boundary between Oregon and Idaho?

🐾 What national park has land along the Pacific Ocean and also inland in the Olympic Mountains? Between what two mountain ranges is the capital of Oregon located?

🐾 Is Seattle, WA, farther north or south of Augusta, ME? (hint: latitude, longitude) What are the chief industries in Washington?

Day 3

🐾 What ocean forms the coastline of Oregon? What is the capital of Oregon?

🐾 In what part of Oregon are the Blue Mountains located? What Oregon lake (the deepest lake in the U.S.) is in the national park that bears its name?

🐾 What is the elevation of Portland, OR? In what city is Oregon's Multnomah County courthouse located?

Day 4

🐾 What is north of Washington? What is the two-letter postal abbreviation for Oregon?

🐾 In which quadrant is Oregon's Mount Hood located; NE, NW, SE, SW? What is the elevation of Mount Rainier?

🐾 What are the chief crops of Oregon? What kind of lumber/timber is grown in Oregon?

POINTS OF INTEREST

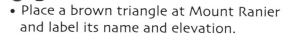

Washington

Mapping

- Draw and label Columbia River.
- Label Canada, Idaho, Oregon, and the Pacific Ocean.
- Label Olympia with a star.

- Shade and label the Olympic Mountains and the Cascade Range.
- Shade and label the Columbia Plateau purple, and label Mount St. Helens.
- Label Strait of Juan de Fuca and Puget Sound.
- Label the Grand Coulee Dam.

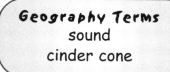

- Place a brown triangle at Mount Ranier and label its name and elevation.
- Draw and label Columbia, Snake, Yakima, and Spokane rivers.
- Label Olympia, Seattle, Spokane, Tacoma, and Walla Walla.

> **Geography Terms**
> sound
> cinder cone

Trail Blazing

As a Matter of Fact...

The San Juan Islands in Puget Sound decrease from 743 to 428 islands between low tide and high tide. Add this and any other interesting "Matter of Fact" to your notebook.

Read about Washington's name, state symbols, and motto. Tell what you learned.

The location of the Cascade Range divides Washington into two extremely diverse climate zones. Study the role climate plays between these two regions. Make a chart depicting the differences in precipitation, temperature, industry, and agriculture in these two zones.

The eruption of Mount St. Helen in 1980 changed the face of the Cascade Range. Learn how it also changed the way some scientists determine the age of the earth.

The Grand Coulee Dam is the third largest electricity producer in the world. Read about its construction and who is beneficiary of its energy. Write or tell about what you learned.

Washington grows more apples than any place in the world. Make a list of all the varieties of apples from Washington. Bake an apple pie or apple crisp for dessert.

Name some famous people from Washington and what they accomplished. Choose one person to write about and include it in your notebook.

Make a timeline of Washington starting in 1775 when Bruno Heceta first landed.

Select from the list of state projects on page 121.

Geography Through Art
Seattle Space Needle

POINTS OF INTEREST

Oregon

Mapping

- Draw and label Columbia River.
- Label Washington, Idaho, Nevada, California, and Pacific Ocean.
- Label Salem with a star.

- Shade and label the Blue Mountains, Cascade Range, and Coast Range.
- Label Harney Basin.
- Shade and label the Columbia Plateau purple.

- Place a brown triangle at Mount Hood and label its name and elevation.
- Shade and label Crater, Goose, Malheur, Harney, and Upper Klamath lakes.
- Draw and label Columbia, Snake, and John Day rivers.
- Label Salem, Portland, and Eugene.

Trail Blazing

As a Matter of Fact...

Beachcombers can still find lumps of beeswax on the coast from the cargo of the *Manzanita*, which sunk there two centuries ago. Add this and any other interesting "Matter of Fact" to your notebook.

Read about Oregon's name, state symbols, and motto. Tell what you learned.

Oregon produces more lumber than any other state. Read about the geography, climate, and natural resources. Tell how each of these are related to one another and how they affect the state's economy.

Study the fertile Willamette River Valley, where most of the people of Oregon live. Write a summary about what you learned. Include what makes the valley fertile and why people have chosen to live there.

There are still visible ruts in some places along the Oregon Trail, a 2000-mile wagon trail from Missouri to the Pacific Coast. Draw the Oregon Trail on a U.S. outline map. Place it in your notebook.

Crater Lake is the deepest lake in the U.S. Learn how it was formed and how deep it is. Write a newspaper article about what you learned.

Name some famous people from Oregon and what they accomplished. Choose one person to write about and include it in your notebook.

Begin to memorize the states and capitals of this region through making flash cards, playing Concentration, or making a crossword puzzle.

Make a timeline of Oregon starting in 1778 when Captain James Cook sailed along the Oregon coast.

Select from the list of state projects on page 121.

GEOGRAPHY TRAILS
Week 29 - Pacific Coast States

Day 1
🐾 What is California's western mountain range called? What lake is located at the border of California and Nevada where both state boundaries bend?

🐾 The San Joaquin River Valley lies between what two mountain ranges? The Colorado River forms the southeast border of California and what other state?

🐾 What is the tallest building in San Francisco, CA, and in what year was its construction completed? How long is the Sacramento River?

Day 2
🐾 What is California's state tree? What is the two-letter postal abbreviation for California?

🐾 Which state has a larger land area: California or Montana? What is California's state nickname?

🐾 What is the lowest point in the U.S. (also the lowest point in North America), and what is its elevation? What California waterfall has a height of around 2425 feet?

Day 3
🐾 What desert is located in the southern part of California? What state shares California's northern boundary?

🐾 If you called your grandma from Disneyland at 5:00 P.M., what time would it be in Ohio where she lives? Where are the San Rafael Mountains located?

🐾 What are California's chief nonfuel minerals? What percentage of the land area in California is used for farming?

Day 4
🐾 What river flows through California's capital city? What body of water is south of the Mojave Desert?

🐾 What is the name of California's famous suspension bridge, and across the entrance to what bay is it located? What is the highest point in California and where is it located?

🐾 What are the chief industries that contribute to California's economy? Which city is farther west: Sacramento or Los Angeles?

POINTS OF INTEREST

California

Mapping

- Draw and label Sacramento River.
- Label Oregon, Nevada, Arizona, Mexico, and the Pacific Ocean.
- Label Sacramento with a star.

- Shade and label the Sierra Nevada Mountains, Coast Ranges, and San Rafael Mountains.
- Shade the Mojave Desert orange, and label Monterey Bay.

- Place a brown triangle at Mount Whitney and label its name and elevation.
- Shade and label Lake Tahoe, Lake Shasta, and the Salton Sea.
- Draw and label Sacramento, Colorado, and San Joaquin rivers.
- Label Oregon, Nevada, Arizona, Mexico, and the Pacific Ocean.
- Label Sacramento, San Francisco, Los Angeles, San Jose, and San Diego.

Trail Blazing

As a Matter of Fact...

Methusela, a 4700-year-old bristlecone pine in Inyo National Forest, is the oldest known living thing in the world. Add this and any other interesting "Matter of Fact" to your notebook.

Read about California's name, state symbols, and motto. Tell what you learned.

California ranks among the top in the U.S. in manufacturing and agriculture. Read about the geography, climate, and natural resources. Tell how each of these are related to one another and how they affect the state's economy. Make a list of California's number ones.

> **Geography Terms** review

Both the lowest and highest points in the continental U.S. states are only 60 miles apart. Learn their names and elevations and locate them on a map of California.

The San Andreas Fault runs 800 miles along California and marks the place where the North American and Northern Pacific tectonic plates meet. Learn about plate tectonics. Tell or write about what you learned. Include a diagram in your notebook.

The Golden Gate Bridge is one of the world's largest suspension bridges. Learn about its construction, maintenance, and use. Write or tell about what you learned.

Name some famous people from California and what they accomplished. Choose one person to write about and include it in your notebook.

Learn the two-letter postal abbreviation of all states in this region.

Make a timeline of California starting in 1542 when Juan Rodriguez Cabrillo explored the San Diego Bay.

Select from the list of state projects on page 121.

GEOGRAPHY TRAILS
— Week 30 - Pacific Coast States —

Day 1

What are the Hawaiian islands made of (how were they formed)? What body of water forms Alaska's northern boundary?

In what national park is the Brooks Range located? What is the northernmost city in Alaska?

The total land area of Alaska is approximately equal to that of Texas and what other three states (list the square miles of each of the four states with your answer)? How many miles of shoreline does Alaska have along the Pacific Ocean?

Day 2

What river spans Alaska from the Canadian border to the Pacific Ocean? What is Alaska's two-letter postal abbreviation?

What is the name given to the stretch of islands running west of the Alaska Peninsula? Is the Kenai Fjords National Park located in the southern or northern part of Alaska?

What are the top three oil producing states? (hint: crude oil) What are the chief manufactured goods of Alaska?

Day 3

What is the capital of Alaska? What is the only U.S. state totally surrounded by water?

What passageway of water connects the Arctic Ocean and the Pacific Ocean and forms the boundary between North America and Asia? What is the southernmost state of the U.S.?

The total land and water area of Hawaii is about the same as what other state? What are the chief crops of Hawaii?

Day 4

What is Hawaii's largest island? What is the capital of Hawaii?

What two Hawaiian islands does the Kauai Channel separate? In which of Hawaii's islands is Pearl Harbor located?

The wettest spot in the world is located in Hawaii; where is it, and what is its annual rainfall? What are the latitude and longitude of Hawaii's capital city?

POINTS OF INTEREST

Alaska

Mapping

- Draw and label Yukon River.
- Label Canada, Arctic Ocean, Russia, and Pacific Ocean.
- Label Juneau with a star.

- Shade and label the Brooks Range and Alaska Range.
- Label Bering Sea, and Bering Strait.
- Label Alaska Peninsula, Alexander Archipelago, and the Aleutian Islands.

- Place a brown triangle at Mount McKinley and label its name and elevation.
- Draw and label Colville, Yukon, Tanana, and Kuskokwim rivers.
- Label Norton Sound, Beaufort Sea, and Kuskokwim Bay.
- Label Juneau, Anchorage, Fairbanks, Sitka, Bethel, and Nome.

Trail Blazing

As a Matter of Fact…

Alaska is one-fifth the size of all the other states together and is so big that the state of Rhode Island could fit into it 425 times! Add this and any other interesting "Matter of Fact" to your notebook.

> **Geography Terms**
> fjord
> strait

Read about Alaska's name, state symbols, and motto. Tell what you learned.

Alaska stretches so far west that the International Date Line is bent around it to keep the whole state in the same day. Learn about time zones and the International Date Line. Practice comparing times in various cities around the world.

There are no roads leading to the state capital. Learn how people get to and from Juneau. Imagine traveling to Juneau from another city in Alaska. Write a journal entry or a letter describing this imaginary trip.

Learn about Alaska's interesting wildlife, including the polar bear, fur seal, moose, and caribou. Tell or write about what you learned. Put pictures in your notebook of at least one animal.

Alaska has an abundance of natural resources, including oil and gold. Read about the geography, climate, and natural resources. Tell how each of these are related to one another and how they affect the state's economy. Take note of the size of fruits and vegetables grown during the 20-hour summer days.

Name some famous people from Alaska and what they accomplished. Choose one person to write about and include it in your notebook.

Review states and capitals of this region.

Make a timeline of Alaska starting in 1741 when Vitus Bering landed on Kayak Island.

Select from the list of state projects on page 121.

Geography Through Art
Eskimo Art – Bone Art

POINTS OF INTEREST

Hawaii

Mapping

- Label each of the Hawaiian Islands: Niihau, Kauai, Oahu, Molokai, Lanai, Maui, Kahoolawe, and Hawaii.
- Label the Pacific Ocean.
- Label Honolulu with a star.

- Label the following channels: Kaulakahi, Kauai, Kaiwi, Kalohi, Kealaikahiki, and Alenuihaha.
- Label Pearl Harbor.

- Place a brown triangle at Mauna Kea and label its name and elevation.
- Label each of the Hawaiian Islands: Niihau, Kauai, Oahu, Molokai, Lanai, Maui, Kahoolawe, and Hawaii.
- Label the Pacific Ocean.
- Label Honolulu, Kailua Kona, Hilo, and Pearl City.

Trail Blazing

As a Matter of Fact...

With an annual rainfall of 460 inches, Mount Waialeale holds the record for being the wettest spot in the world. Add this and any other interesting "Matter of Fact" to your notebook.

> **Geography Terms**
> volcano
> channel

Read about Hawaii's name, state symbols, and motto. Tell what you learned.

Hawaiian beaches can be black or white. Learn what substances create the different colors.

Tourism is Hawaii's largest industry, yet it also leads the nation in producing bananas, guavas, macadamia nuts, papaya, coffee, and pineapples. Read about the geography, climate, and natural resources. Tell how each of these are related to one another and how they affect the state's economy.

Hawaii has the most diverse ethnic mix of any state. Many of the natives are descendants of the Polynesians. Read about the island of Niihau which has strictly limited public access, allowing the pure-blooded Hawaiians to speak their own language and keep their native traditions. Write a summary of what you learned and put it in your notebook.

The Hawaiian Islands are actually the cone-shaped tops of undersea volcanoes, and some are active today. Learn about volcanoes. Write or tell what you learned.

The island of Kauai is known for its tropical gardens and the beautiful Waimea Canyon. Obtain a travel brochure and learn more about this island. Make a list of flowers and other plants grown there.

Hawaii is not actually located in North America, but in Polynesia, a part of Oceania. Make a list of Polynesian islands.

Make a timeline of Hawaii starting in 1778 when Captain James Cook explored it.

Select from the list of state projects on page 121.

The Lewis and Clark Expedition
May 1804-September 1806

Commissioned by his friend and boss, President Thomas Jefferson, Meriwether Lewis was to find the Northwest Passage to the Pacific Ocean and record all new discoveries along the way. Lewis chose William Clark as an equal partner in leadership in what is perhaps the most successful exploration of our land ever attempted. The 31 members of the Corps of Discovery, left from the Wood River, traveled over 8000 miles of uncharted territory on foot, on horseback, by boat, and upriver, over the Rocky Mountains to the Pacific Ocean, and lost only one man (from natural causes). Not only did they chart maps of this new land (Clark), but they also discovered and recorded over 170 new plants and 125 new animals for science (Lewis). They developed friendly relations with nearly 50 tribes of Native Americans over the two-and-one-half-year expedition.

During the next six weeks study the Lewis and Clark Expedition by using the book *The Captain's Dog*. Choose from an assortment of weekly assignments and either develop a separate notebook or include the study in a section of the State Notebook already begun. Feel free to use other resources to add to your study. A few suggestions are listed with recommended resources.

Reading Aloud
This book is good for family read aloud time. To complete this study in six weeks follow the weekly reading plan. Since *The Captain's Dog* does not use chapter numbers, weekly reading is assigned by Lewis's journal entry dates. Page numbers from First Gulliver Books 2000 copyright paperback edition are listed in parentheses. Questions for discussion are followed by the answer and page number where the answer can be found. The discussion questions are by no means comprehensive so feel free to offer your own topics for discussion.

Mapping
Use an outline map of the United States for the mapping assignments. You will need at least three copies. Mapping assignments are labeled according to levels. Secondary level will do all the mapping. Intermediate will do most of the mapping. Be sure to use the map in the front matter of the novel as a ready reference to keep track of where the Corps travels along the journey.

Trail Blazing Levels
To aid you in choosing assignments for Trail Blazing, projects are listed in order from simplest to most difficult. Choose projects for Primary level from the first two or three listed, Intermediate from the middle and Secondary from the middle to the end.

The Captain's Dog, My Journey with the Lewis and Clark Tribe by Roland Smith
This story begins on a vast prairie in 1808 with a reunion of old friends and fellow explorers. John Colter and George Drouillard (pronounced sort of like Drewyer) had arrived with furs they intended to trade with the Indians. To their delight they see Seaman, Meriwether Lewis's Newfoundland dog, who obviously had not died during the return home of their courageous expedition as they had thought. Seaman's new owners were a couple of Indian friends they had made on that famous journey. In the 2–3-day wait to trade, they are asked by their Indian friends to read from a peculiar red book in their possession. To their surprise the book turns out to be the personal diary of Captain

Lewis written during the fantastic journey in which these old friends had survived a couple of years before. Thus the story unfolds of the most magnificent exploration of the United States ever attempted. Travel with the explorers through the journal entries and reminiscences, but mostly through the eyes of Seaman, who saw it all firsthand.

Please Note:
Disobedient crew members were sternly punished. Harsh punishments were customary on ships as discipline and line of authority is key to any successful voyage or exploration. One particular scene could be disturbing to young children. It is found on page 27 (or if page numbers change in future printings of the novel - after the journal entry of July 4). You may want to skip this part when reading to young students. If so, mark it in pencil in the book before you begin reading.

In addition, the author chose to express frustration by a key character by including a curse. If you want to substitute your own word or leave this out completely mark it in advance of the reading. This is on page 275 (or if page numbers change in future printings - after the section dated July 26, 1806).

About the Author
Roland Smith was a biologist for over 20 years, specializing in canines. As an author it was natural for him to write this story from Seaman's perspective. Other children's books written by Roland Smith include: *Sasquatch, Jaguar,* and *Thunder Cave.*

Recommended resources:
- *The Captain's Dog, My Journey with the Lewis and Clark Tribe* by Roland Smith (Gulliver Books Harcourt, Inc., ISBN:0-15-202696-7)
- United States outline map (*Uncle Josh's Outline Map Book* or CD-ROM)
- *Children's Illustrated Atlas of the United States*
- Colored pencils
- Library books or other research resources

Optional:
- U.S. historical atlas with the Lewis and Clark route marked
- U.S. road atlas (for finding places along the Missouri River where Lewis and Clark traveled)
- *National Geographic* Feb. 2003 issue (great article on Sacajawea and the expedition)
- PBS documentary: *Lewis and Clark: The Journey of the Corps of Discovery* by Ken Burns

Optional additional reading material:
  The Incredible Journey of Lewis and Clark by Rhoda Blumberg (info, sketches, and pictures)
  The Adventures of Lewis and Clark, by John Bakeless (historical fiction)
  Across America by Jacqueline Morley

Websites:
There are literally hundreds of websites devoted to this topic. Key "Lewis and Clark" into your Internet browser or use the links provided on the websites listed below.
  www.nationalgeographic.com
  www.lewisandclark.org
  www.lewis-clark.org

Read: The beginning through August 11, 1804 (3-50)

What animals did they take with them? (Seaman and two horses, p.10) On what form of transportation did the crew travel? (two pirogues and one keelboat, p.10) How did the men get the boats upriver during days when the wind blew against their intended direction? (by towing the boats with ropes while walking along the shore, p.11) What route did Captain Lewis tell Seaman's owner he intended to take to the Pacific Ocean? (down the Ohio, up the Mississippi, up the Missouri, and on, p.17) Who was Dorion? (a trader with knowledge of the Sioux, p.22) How was the poultice of Peruvian bark used? (to treat snake bite, p.30) What compensation were the men who completed the expedition promised? (400-acre land grant, p.34) Who was a troublemaker? (Reed, p.34) Who chose his friendships poorly? (Newman, p.34) What was Captain Clark's birthday dinner? (venison, roasted beaver tail, elk steak, berries, p.36) What gifts did the Oto Indians prefer to receive? (gunpowder and whiskey, p.45) What happened to the Omaha Nation? (died from smallpox, p.48)

Mapping

- Label Pittsburgh, PA, where Lewis bought Seaman.
- Label Clarksville (IN) and Council Bluffs (IA).
- Locate France and Spain on a globe or map of the world.
- Draw and label the Wood, Ohio, Mississippi, and Missouri Rivers.

Trail Blazing

List the plants and animals you read about each week.

List the Indian tribes you read about each week.

Start a list of the collections. This week: rattlesnake rattle, rattlesnake skin, and badger.

Select one Indian tribe and learn about its people, or start a sheet of Indian customs. Make a list of each Indian tribe as you meet them, and record their customs or ways of getting food, building houses etc.

Start a list showing the different skills and characteristics of both Captain Lewis and Captain Clark. Add to it throughout the story. Notice how each contributed to the success of this mission.

Read about the pirogue. Write a paragraph telling what you learned. Include a drawing.

What did you think of the court martial of Collins and Hall? Was the punishment of 100 lashes and back to work the next day too harsh, or was it necessary? Watch for further disciplinary action the men received and see if by the end of this book you think strict discipline was necessary. Learn about the procedure for court martial in today's military.

Describe the character and personality of York. Tell what you admire about him and how you would feel if you were in his position.

Vocabulary

pirogue   poultice   prairie

Read: August 15, 1804 through November 3, 1804 (51-93)

What was the net made of that caught nearly 800 fish? (willow bark, p.51) What were the "whistling rats"? (prairie dogs, p.68) What did Shannon use for ammunition when he ran out of balls for his musket? (he whittled a piece of wood to form a ball, p.70) What supplies did the Corps obtain from the Arikara tribe? (corn, tobacco, buffalo robes, p.77) Who wanted to mutiny, and who influenced him? (Newman was influenced by Reed, p.80) How did Newman respond to his punishment? (changed and recanted, p.81) Who was added to the group at Fort Mandan and why? (Charbonneau as a boatman and his wife, Sacajawea, to interpret Shoshone, p.92)

Mapping

• Draw and label Floyd's River and Knife River.
• Label the Fort Mandan Village.

Trail Blazing

List the plants and animals you read about this week.

List the Indian tribes you read about this week.

List what foods the explorers ate.

Add to your list of the collections: prairie wolf and prairie dog.

Compare the Teton Sioux and the Yankton Sioux people. Write a paragraph on each. See if you can find a picture of these tribes or of their handiwork to include in your notebook.

Learn about keelboats. Summarize your study in a paragraph and include a drawing.

Learn more about Meriwether Lewis and his preparations to lead this journey.

Sgt. Floyd died of a ruptured appendix. It is believed that he would have suffered the same fate had he been home when this occurred. Study appendicitis, its symptoms, and how it is treated today.

In addition to both Lewis and Clark, many others on this perilous journey kept journals of their experiences. Start a journal of your own as though you are a member of the Corps of Discovery and make regular entries during the next five weeks.

Captain Lewis gave a speech to each new tribe they encountered. Write a speech that he could have given. Use the same ideas he included in his presentation and present the speech yourself.

Make beef jerky. (See recipe online at http://www.fabulousfoods.com/recipes/misc/jerky.html)

Study the musket rifle. Learn how it loads and fires. Include a drawing or picture of a musket in your notebook.

Vocabulary
flanks   blunderbuss

Read: Jan 12, 1805 through June 9, 1805 (94-139)

When food became scarce how did the men get food? (traded with Indians for medical care, p.95) Who is Bird Woman and what happened with her at Fort Mandan? (nickname for Sacajawea, gave birth to Jean Baptiste, whom Clark called Pomp, p.97) On March 30, 1805 they headed into uncharted territory and sent information gathered up to this point to what president? (Jefferson, p.101) How many miles per day did they expect to travel? (25, p.101) What transportation did they establish for this leg of the journey? (two pirogues and six dugout canoes rigged with sails, p.101) What did Bird Woman take from the mice nest? (peanuts – but she left some for the mice! p. 103) Who saved valuable papers from the boating mishap? (Bird Woman, p.118) Was Charbonneau as good a boatman as he had said he was? (no, p.118) How did Charbonneau get back into the good graces of Captain Meriwether? (prepared his favorite meal – boudin blanc, made of buffalo sausage, p.119) What animal charged through the camp while Charbonneau was on sentry duty? (buffalo, p.126) How did Captain Lewis respond to Windsor's predicament? (calm, confident, encouraging – qualities of a true leader, p.135)

Mapping

- Draw and label Yellowstone River (near the end of the Missouri River).
- Draw and label Maria's River (right Branch of the Missouri).
- Using a fresh U.S. map, draw and shade the Louisiana Purchase.

Trail Blazing

List the plants and animals you read about this week.

What foods did the explorers eat?

Learn about beavers and how they build their dams. Include a picture in your notebook.

Look at pictures of the Rocky Mountains. Write a letter home as though you were one of the men on the journey telling about your first sight of the Rocky Mountains.

Study grizzly bears. Learn about their habitat, hibernation, average size, diet, and more. Make a poster with pictures showing what you have learned.

Study the Louisiana Purchase. Learn the who, what, when, where, and why of this acquisition. Write a summary and include it in your notebook.

Choke cherry bark (or its branch) relieved Captain Lewis' severe stomach pains, and he was able to walk 30 miles the next day! Study the medicinal use of herbs and plants. Make a simple remedy booklet choosing 4-6 common ailments. With your parent's permission, obtain herbs at your local health food store, and try a natural remedy when the opportunity arises.

Study the presidency of Thomas Jefferson. Include his goals and accomplishments, and name some people he relied upon to bring success to his term of office.

Vocabulary

forge	squall	whelping (time)
dugouts (p. 113)	cache	espontoon

Read: June 13, 1805 through August 8, 1805 (140-186)

What did Captain Lewis value more than the beautiful sight at Great Falls? (that the men followed him despite their reservations, p.141) How far was the portage around the falls? (16 miles, p.147) What were some of the hindrances to this portage? (weather, ruts, prickly pear, hai, p.150) What kind of preparation did the men make after making the portage? (made canoes, sewed new moccasins, dried meat, and packed supplies, p.159) Why did the Shoshone Indian turn and ride away? (Shields was not paying attention and scared him away, p.182) How did Lewis make known to the Shoshone warrior that they were friendly? (waved the American flag over his head, and had the old woman and two girls follow him; red painted faces meant peace, p.185) How did Cameahwait show the captain he was friendly? (tied small sea shells in their hair, p.186)

Mapping

- Label Great Falls, MT.
- Trace and label Madison, Jefferson, Medicine, and Gallatin Rivers.
- Label White Bear Island (use your best guess).
- Find and label Three Forks.
- Find and label Beaver's Head.

Trail Blazing

List the plants and animals you read about this week.

List the Indian tribes you read about this week.

Keep track of the foods the explorers ate.

Draw the American flag as it looked in 1805. Include it in your notebook.

The group celebrated their second Fourth of July since their departure. Learn more about this holiday which we still observe today. How does your family spend this day?

Read about the Shoshone Indian tribe and tell what you thought was most interesting.

Learn about flash floods and what conditions lead to flash flooding. Make a poster with flash flood safety instructions.

Clark showed great diplomacy with Lewis when the iron boat was a failure. Discuss how to treat one another when someone is prideful or experiences failure.

Learn more about William Clark and his role in this successful journey. Learn about his accomplishments after this adventure and how he further served his country.

Learn about the various ways seeds are dispersed. Write a report and include names of plants and the dispersal method of their seeds.

Vocabulary

precipice   portage   swamp(y)   vermilion

Read: August 15, 1805 through September 22, 1805 (187-242)

What disturbing news did Captain Lewis learn from Cameahwait? (There is no Northwest Passage, p.189) What was the boldest thing Captain Lewis instructed his men to do in an effort to convince the Shoshone they were not headed for an ambush? (He told his men to give their guns to the Indians, p.196) Why did Old Toby's sons turn back? (to provide buffalo meat for their families, p.206) How did the Flathead, Three Eagles, know the explorers were friendly? (by their casual way of travel and because they traveled with a woman and child, p.208) How did the group get so spread out in their trek through the Rockies? (travel difficulties through snow, ravines, terrain, and falls required repacking supplies, p.214) Who chastened the Nez Percé for discussing evil against the white? (Watkuweis "...bad talk leads to bad actions...," p.231) Finally they reach the Pacific Ocean! How many miles was the trip? (4142 miles, p.238)

🐾 Mapping

𝖄𝖄. Label Traveler's Rest.

𝖄𝖄. Draw and label Clearwater, Snake, and Columbia Rivers.

𝖄𝖄. Label Celilo Falls and Cape Disappointment.

𝖄𝖄. Label Fort Clatsop.

- Look at a map and locate the Cape of Good Hope at the tip of South America. Trace the trip people would take from the Columbia River to the East Coast if they had found a ship to take their papers.

Trail Blazing

Communication from English to French to Hiaatsa to Shoshone must have been a difficult task. To see for yourself make up a silly sentence and whisper it to one person in the room. Have that person whisper the sentence to another person in the room until it has passed through four people. See how close the fourth person comes to repeating the original silly sentence.

Imagine you were a member of the expedition. Write a journal entry for the day you finally arrived at the Pacific Ocean.

What foods did the explorers find to eat? Food became so scarce that they had to resort to desperate measures to eat. Have you ever been so hungry you thought you'd starve? Describe your experience. You may want to try to skip a meal or two to see if you can begin to understand their hunger. Be sure to get permission before you try this activity.

Read about the Nez Percé and the Flathead Indian tribes. Learn about their culture, or typical daily life. Add to the sheet of Indian customs.

What did Seaman mean by, "It was like dropping a pebble into a dry well"? (pg. 193) See how many ways you can describe the same feeling using other comparisons.

This week we learn that the primary objective the journey could not be fulfilled, since there was actually no Northwest Passage after all. How did Lewis and Clark react to this news? Write about each man's reaction. How would you hope to respond to such disappointment?

Vocabulary

harangue	indolence	ravine	plateau	estuary

Read: January 1, 1806 to the end (243-283)

What did Bird Woman insist upon seeing on the beach? (a beached whale, p.245) Who celebrated his first birthday? (Pomp, p.246) During the winter, what did Lewis and Clark do with their time? (Lewis worked on his animal collections and Clark on his maps, p.244) When did they begin their return trip home, and how long had it been since they had entered uncharted territory? (The return began March 23, 1806 - they had left charted territory March 30, 1805 – one year earlier, p.249) Who did the Nez Percé call the "white healer"? (Clark, p.254) What were some of the reasons for the first retreat? (left Nez Percé camp too early – too much snow, not enough food for animals, Potts' injury, p.260) Why were the guides reluctant to take the men to Maria's River? (Blackfoot Indian territory, they feared the Blackfeet, p.266) How did Mountain Dog and Watsukeis end up with Captain Lewis' dog and the journal? (Tell in your own words.)

Mapping

• Trace the return trip from the Columbia River to the place where Lewis and Clark separated.

• Mark both captains' routes (Clark – to the Jefferson River to Three Forks to Yellowstone. Lewis to Great Falls to Maria's River to Yellowstone) then on to the Missouri.

Trail Blazing

List the Indian tribes you read about this week.

Study the Blackfoot Indians and their culture, or add to the sheet of Indian customs.

What are hot springs? What causes them? Read and report on what you learn.

Sacajawea contributed much to the Lewis and Clark Expedition, but not as an interpreter and guide as is often reported. Find out what role her presence on this journey did play. (Feb. 2003 *National Geographic* has a good article and wonderful pictures.)

Explain the circumstances behind the death of the young Blackfoot. Do you think this could have been avoided? Lewis had been warned not to go up the Maria's River, yet he did and it was filled with disaster. Tell of a time you were warned about something but did it anyway. What were the results from your circumstance?

Read any other additional books and material you may have gathered about the Corps of Discovery. Write a summary of what the Lewis and Clark Expedition accomplished.

Finalize any projects and research. Organize your notebook. Look over the lists you made from reading this novel.

View the PBS documentary *Lewis and Clark: The Journey of the Corps of Discovery* by Ken Burns, or National Geographic's large, format (IMAX) film *"Lewis and Clark: Great Journey West."* Did the book *The Captain's Dog* tell the same story as the video?

Appendix

Project Choices and Formulas
A Student Reference Sheet

To add interest to your geography studies, select from these projects. Copy this page and place it in your notebook to use as a handy reference. Project ideas are separated by whether they apply more to the region or state. Use your own judgment. If you want to do a crossword for the state or a word search for the region, go for it! Instructions begin on page 13.

Regional Projects

Crossword Puzzle
Salt Dough Map
Climate
Face the Facts
Flash Cards
Memory (Concentration)

State Projects

States of the Union
Signature State
State Your Questions
Word Search
Go Team Go!
Travel Brochure
Economy
Flags
Eat Your Way Through the USA

 Formulas

Students following the bear track and using an almanac as your main reference will find these formulas helpful. After you have used them a few times, try to answer the questions without referring to the formula hints.

What % of land is forested?

% of forested land = $\dfrac{\text{forested land area}}{\text{total land area}}$ X 100

What % of land is farm land?

% of farm land = $\dfrac{\text{farm land area}}{\text{total land area}}$ X 100

What % of planted land was harvested?

% of harvested land = $\dfrac{\text{harvested land}}{\text{planted land area}}$ X 100

> Note: You must use the same unit of measure for area. If the almanac provides one in acres and one in square miles, convert the acres to square miles. There are 640 acres in every square mile of land. To convert acres to square miles divide by 640.
>
> square miles = $\dfrac{\text{acres}}{640}$

What % of U.S. potatoes are grown in Idaho?

% of U.S. potatoes from Idaho = $\dfrac{\text{amount of Idaho potatoes}}{\text{amount of total U.S. potatoes}}$ X 100

What % of land is federally owned land?

% of federally owned land = $\dfrac{\text{federal land area}}{\text{total land area}}$ X 100

Population Density = $\dfrac{\text{population}}{\text{total land area}}$

_____   # Timeline
state name

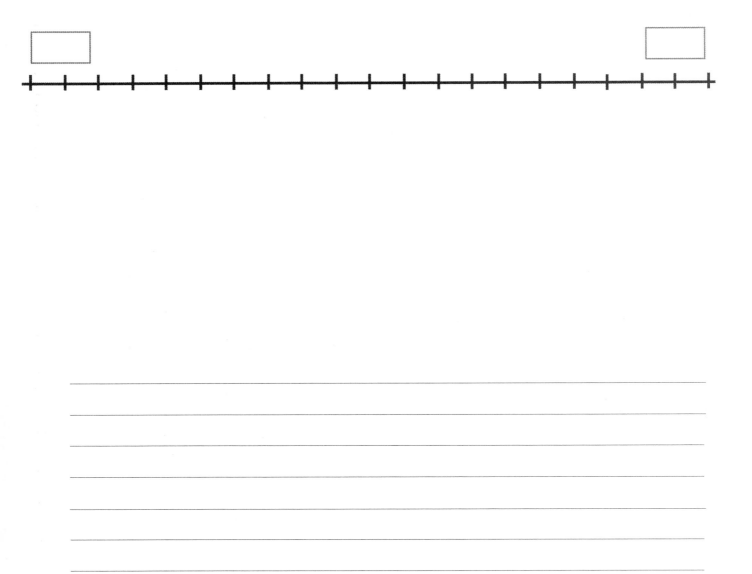

Make a two-sided copy of this page for each state. Put dates in the boxes and anywhere in between you choose. Record information with text, figures, or drawings. Describe other interesting facts on lower lines.

©2007 Geography Matters

States of the Union

_____
state

_____
abbreviation

Darken the correct state.

State Nickname: _____

State Motto: _____

Date of Statehood: _____

Rank (by date): _____

Capital: _____

Largest City (by population): _____

Land Area (square miles): _____

Highest Elevation: _____

Main Rivers: _____
_____

Leading Products: _____
_____

State Bird

Significant People and What They Did

State Flower

Important Events in the State's History

State Tree

©2007 Geography Matters

Time Zone Map

Hawaii-Aleutian -10	Alaska -9	Pacific -8	Mountain -7	Central -6	Eastern -5

Alaska

Instructions for use:

The world is divided into 24 time zones, starting with the zero meridian or Prime Meridian (near Greenwich, England). Each 15° rotation of the earth takes about an hour. Time zones west of the Prime Meridian are earlier and marked with a minus, and time zones east are later than Greenwich Mean Time and are marked with a plus.

To determine the time from one time zone to another follow this simple formula: add one hour for each time zone heading in the easterly direction, or subtract one hour for each time zone heading in the westerly direction. For example, you live in the Central Standard time zone and want to determine the time of someone in the Pacific Standard time zone: the time you seek is two hours in the westerly direction so simply subtract two hours from your time.

Pacific

Mountain

Central

Eastern

Hawaii-Aleutian

©2007 Geography Matters

Go Team, Go!

Team Logo

Team Name _____

City _____

Sport _____

Coach _____

Mascot _____

Favorite Players

Player _____   Player _____

Position _____   Position _____

Stats _____   Stats _____

_____   _____

1. What is the championship of this sport called?

_____

2. Has this team ever won it?_____

3. Why do you think the name, logo or mascot was chosen for this team? _____

4. Name museums or other places of interest in this city.

_____

_____

_____

©2007 Geography Matters

Go Team, Go!

[Team Logo]

Team Name _____

City _____

Sport _____

Coach _____

Mascot _____

Favorite Players

Player _____   Player _____

Position _____   Position _____

Stats_____   Stats _____

_____   _____

1. What is the championship of this sport called?
   _____

2. Has this team ever won it?_____   When?_____

3. What borders this state to the West? _____

   East? _____   South?_____   North?_____

4. Professional and college sports teams are found in cities with strong support such as many fans, big stadiums, etc.

   What is the population of this city? _____

   Is it the largest city in the state? _____

   What does the community do to help this team?

   _____

   _____

   _____

   _____

©2007 Geography Matters

_____
state

State Your Questions

1. In what region is this state located? _____

   _____

2. What is the state capital? _____

3. What is the state nickname ? _____

   _____

4. What is the state motto? _____

   _____

5. What bodies of water are in and near this state?

   _____

   _____

6. What do you notice about this state? _____

   _____

   _____

   _____

   _____

   _____

Add your own questions.

©2007 Geography Matters

<u>   </u>
state

State Your Questions

1. What is the climate?

_____

2. What are the main crops grown in this state?

_____

3. What products and businesses is this state known for?

_____

_____

4. What are the most popular tourist attractions?

_____

_____

5. What forms the boundaries of this state on the north, east, south, and west?

_____

_____

_____

6. In what time zone(s) is this state located?

_____

_____

_____

_____

_____

_____

Add your own questions.

©2007 Geography Matters

_____
state

State Your Questions

1. What principal crops are grown in this state?

_____

_____

2. What industries help form the economy?

_____

3. What is the history of this state entering the union?

_____

_____

_____

4. What are the national parks, national monuments, and national landmarks?

_____

_____

5. What plants and animals are found here? Are any special to this area only?

_____

_____

6. In what time zone(s) is this state located?

_____

7. What are the area of this state and its rank by size?_____

_____

_____

_____

_____

_____

_____

Add your own questions.

©2007 Geography Matters

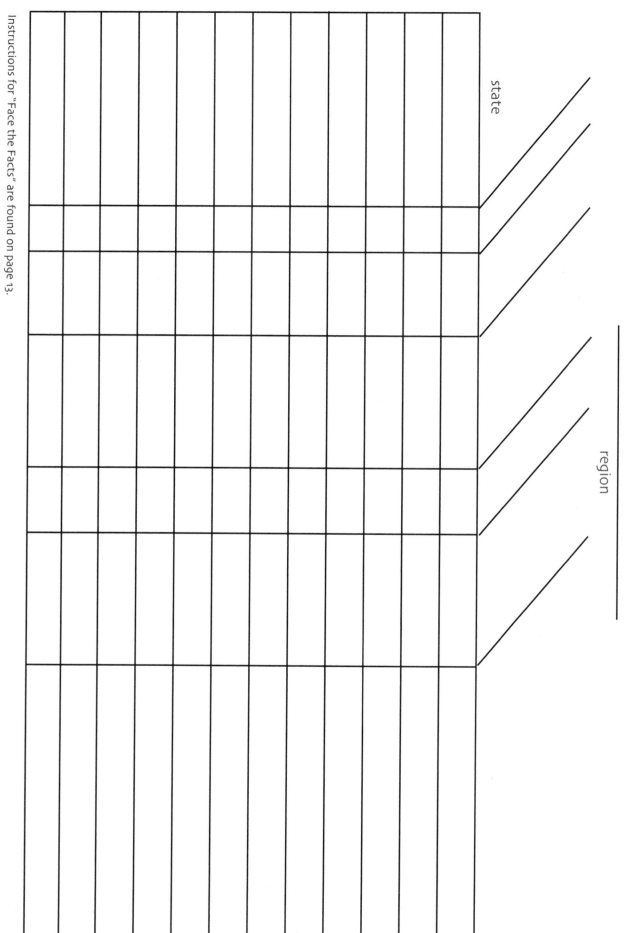

Face the Facts

state

region

Instructions for "Face the Facts" are found on page 13.

Illustrated Geography Dictionary

©2007 Geography Matters

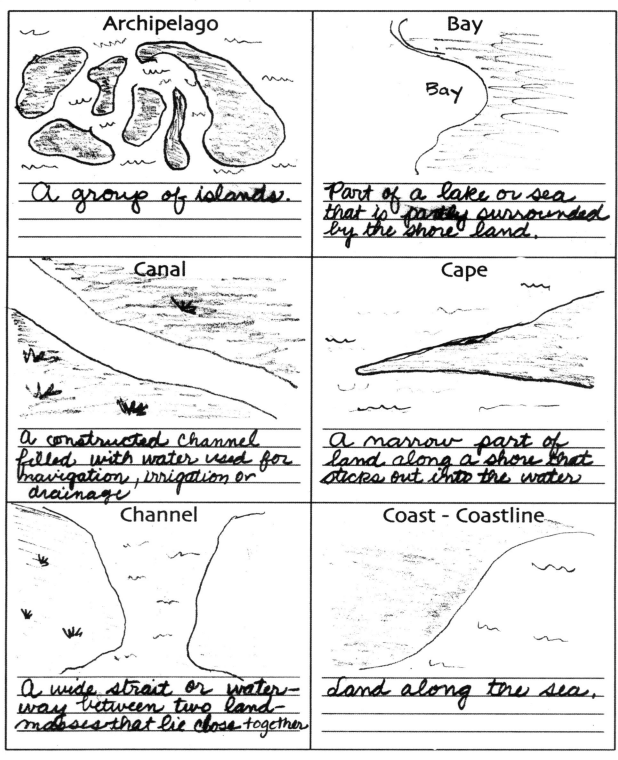

Archipelago

A group of islands.

Bay

Part of a lake or sea that is partly surrounded by the shore land.

Canal

A constructed channel filled with water used for navigation, irrigation or drainage

Cape

A narrow part of land along a shore that sticks out into the water

Channel

A wide strait or waterway between two landmasses that lie close together

Coast - Coastline

Land along the sea.

Sample Illustrated Dictionary Page

ANSWERS

Week 1

1-Augusta; Canada
2-Katahdin Mountains; Atlantic Ocean
3-Boston; Vermont, New Hampshire
4-Boston Bay; Cape Cod

1-chickadee; Kennebec, Penobscot, or St. Croix Rivers
2-Kennebec; New Hampshire
3-western part of the state; Charles River
4-New Hampshire, Vermont, New York, Connecticut, Rhode Island; Mount Greylock (3487 feet)

1-Land area is 30,995 square miles (total area is 35,385); potatoes
2-Bangor, Portland; Acadia National Park
3-temperate, with colder and drier climate in the western region; "By the sword we seek peace, but peace only under liberty"
4-Bay State; Merrimack River, Connecticut River, Housatonic River, Concord River, Charles River

Week 2

1-Atlantic Ocean; purple finch
2-Merrimack River; Canada
3-Green Mountains (in the Appalachians); Massachusetts
4-Lake Champlain; Montpelier

1-Franklin, Concord, Manchester, Nashua; 2:00 P.M.
2-Mount Washington (6288 ft.); Umbagog Lake
3-Lake Champlain; Vermont
4-Otter River; Massachusetts

1-all (coast, hills and mountains, and plateau); tourism, manufacturing, agriculture, trade, and mining
2-8968 square miles; its nearness to the high mountains and ocean
3-Vermont; dairy products, apples, maple syrup, greenhouse/nursery, vegetables, and small fruits
4-mountainous or forest (Vermont is three-fourths forest land); Green Mountain

Week 3

1-Hartford; New York, Massachusetts, and Rhode Island
2-Housatonic River; white oak
3-Atlantic Ocean; Jerimoth Hill (elevation 812 feet)
4-Block Island; Providence

1-Connecticut River; Quinnipiac River and Housatonic River
2-forests; Mount Frissell (elevation 2380 feet)
3-Rhode Island, Prudence Island, Conaicut Island, to name a few; Blackstone River and Providence River
4-40 miles; Narragansett Bay

1-New Haven, Bridgeport, and New London; moderate winters, average slightly below freezing, with warm, humid summers.
2-aircraft engines, submarines, helicopters, machinery, computer equipment, and electronics, to name a few; "He who transplants, still sustains."
3-50th; eastern lowlands of the Narragansett Basin, western uplands of flat and rolling hills.
4-Providence, Rhode Island; services and manufacturing

ANSWERS

Week 4

1-New York; Charleston
2-Lake Ontario; Appalachian Mountains
3-Hudson River; New Jersey, Maryland, Pennsylvania
4-Maryland; Delaware River

1-Trenton, NJ; New York
2-Delaware Bay; New York
3-Lake Erie; Pine Barrens
4-Long Island Sound; Mount Marcy (5344 feet) in New York

1-3rd largest; apples, grapes, strawberries, cherries, and pears
2-*54%; New York, Buffalo, and Albany
3-pharmaceuticals/drugs, telecommunications, biotechnology, printing & publishing; Coastal Plain
4-New Jersey; pine, cedar, and mixed hardwood

* % of forested land =

$$\frac{\text{forested land area}}{\text{total land area}} \times 100$$

$$\text{square miles} = \frac{\text{acres}}{640}$$

Week 5

1-Pennsylvania; Harrisburg
2-Atlantic Ocean; Potomac River
3-cardinal; Chesapeake Bay
4-New York, New Jersey, Maryland, West Virginia, Ohio, Delaware; sugar maple

1-Hudson River; west
2-New River Gorge; Mount Davis (3213 feet)
3-Susquehanna River; Mountain State
4-Pymatuning Reservoir and Allegheny Reservoir; Virginia

1-continental climate with wide fluctuations in seasonal temperatures; Philadelphia, Pittsburgh, and Erie
2-cattle, sheep, hogs, and chickens; 6th
3-Allegheny Plateau; lower
4-machinery, plastic and hardwood products, fabricated metals, chemicals, aluminum automotive parts, and steel; oak, yellow poplar, hickory, walnut, and cherry

Week 6

1-New Jersey; Albany
2-New York; Ohio River
3-blue hen chicken; MD
4-Dover; Delaware Bay

1-Chesapeake and Delaware Canal; Rehoboth Bay and Indian River Bay
2-1955 square miles, ranked 49th; Chesapeake Bay
3-Pennsylvania and Maryland; Maryland
4-8 P.M.; Backbone Mountain (3360 feet)

1-greenhouse and nursery products, soybeans, and corn; black-eyed Susan
2-humid subtropical; higher
3-Piedmont Plateau to the north, sloping to a near sea-level plain; moderate
4-32%; over 400 people per square mile

 Please Note:
The secondary level answers could vary from year to year, depending upon what year almanac is used. Most answers were obtained from a 2007 almanac.

ANSWERS

Week 7

1-Kennebec River; VT
2-black-capped chickadee; Atlantic Ocean
3-American elm; Trenton
4-MD; Appalachian Mountains

1-Massachusetts and Rhode Island; Maryland, Vermont, New Hampshire, New Jersey (in this order)
2-eastern; south
3-New Jersey; Delaware
4-Allegheny River, Monongahela River; western

1-Pennsylvania; Maine, New Hampshire
2-Delaware; New York
3-Maine; more than 10,000 people per square mile
4-05855; Hartford

Week 8

1-Richmond; South Carolina
2-Atlantic Ocean; Savannah River
3-cardinal; North Carolina
4-Appalachian Mountains; Virginia

1-Atlantic Ocean and Chesapeake Bay; Mount Rogers (5729 feet), located in the Appalachian Mountains near the North Carolina border
2-Great Smoky Mountains National Park; Piedmont (Piedmont Plateau)
3-Lake Marion and Lake Moultrie; Georgia
4-Brasstown Bald (4784 feet), located in the Appalachian Mountains near the North Carolina Border; Attamaha River

1-highest point is Mount Mitchell in Yancy county, elevation 6684, lowest point is sea level at the Atlantic Ocean; 112 miles
2-430 miles long and 200 miles wide; NC
3-less than; 48 inches per year
4-110° F, July 15, 1954; mild and equable

Week 9

1-KY; Nashville
2-Kentucky Lake; Appalachian Mountains
3-dogwood tree; NC
4-Ohio River; cardinal

1-Mammoth Cave National Park; hilly
2-Cumberland Plateau; Clingman's Dome (6643 feet), located in the Great Smoky Mountain National Park
3-48,718 square miles and ranked 29th; Cape Hatteras
4-James River, Rappahannock River, York River; Shenandoah National Park

1-one; Kentucky
2-tobacco; highest elevation at Clingman's Dome 6643 feet high, lowest at the Mississippi River elevation at 178 feet
3-it was -37°F on Jan. 19,1994; May
4-KY and TN; KY

ANSWERS

Week 10

1-Columbia; Florida
2-GA; Florida
3-brown thrasher;
   Chattahoochee River
4-palmetto; central

1-Sassafras Mountain (3560 feet) in the northwest corner of the state; 30,111 square miles, ranks 40th
2-3 P.M.; Chattahoochee River
3-south of Florida Bay in the Atlantic Ocean, south and west of the peninsula of Florida (answers will vary); Biscayne National Park and Everglades National Park
4-Kissimmee River; Tampa Bay

1-clays, crushed stone, cement, sand and gravel; fourth
2-300 miles long and 239 miles wide; Georgia
3-August 21, 1983; South Carolina, Georgia, Florida (in this order); 110°
4-52 inches per year; less

Week 11

1-Alabama; Mississippi, Alabama, and Georgia
2-Little Rock; Gulf of Mexico
3-AR; Louisiana
4-eastern brown pelican; Missouri River

1-Magazine Mountain (2753 feet) southeast of Ft. Smith (answers will vary); Texas
2-Lake Pontchartrain; southern because it is surrounded by water from the Gulf of Mexico at sea level
3-Cheaha Mountain (4205 feet) located in the Appalachian Mountains west of Georgia (answers will vary); Mobile Bay
4-Pearl River; 46,914 square miles, ranked 31st

1-less; Arkansas
2-61°F high and 40°F low; corn
3-Alabama; higher
4-Pascagoula, MS; April

Please Note:
The secondary level answers could vary from year to year, depending upon what year almanac is used. Most answers were obtained from a 2007 almanac.

Week 12

1-Gulf of Mexico; Alabama
2-Georgia and Alabama; Louisiana
3-FL; yellowhammer
4-Lake Okeechobee; Jacksonville

1-New Orleans, LA; Mississippi and Alabama
2-53,937 square miles; Apalachee Bay
3-Gulf coast; Alabama
4-Charlotte Harbor; Driskill Mountain (535 feet) located in the north central part of the state (answer may vary)

1-Florida; Gulf coast
2-Tampa; tourism, agriculture, manufacturing, construction, services, international trade
3-FL; phosphate rock, crushed stone, cement, and sand and gravel
4-more than; Florida

ANSWERS

Week 13

1-Arkansas River; Arkansas and Louisiana
2-Arkansas; Arkansas
3-Tennessee River; Tennessee River
4-Cumberland River; Baton Rouge

1-Louisiana; New Orleans, LA
2-Mississippi; Louisiana
3-Arkansas; Woodall Mountain, located in the northeast corner of the state
4-Memphis; east

1-soybeans; 260 miles long and 240 miles wide
2-Ouachita River (55 feet above sea level); 49 inches
3-397 miles of coastline and 7721 of shoreline; Louisiana
4-elevation 8 ft below sea level in New Orleans; Lousiana

Week 14

1-Gulf of Mexico; Ouachita Mountains
2-tulip poplar; Cape Fear River
3-no; VA
4-Chattahoochee River; Jackson

1-the Piedmont; Durham, Chapel Hill, and Raleigh
2-Louisville; Arkansas
3-Tennessee and North Carolina; peanuts
4-Virginia; Frankfort, KY

1-Virginia; New York
2-Alabama, South Carolina, Tennessee
3-Kentucky; Arkansas
4-Florida, Louisiana; import

Week 15

1-Ohio; Ohio River
2-Lower Peninsula; Wolverine State
3-OH; Michigan
4-Lake Erie; Ohio

1-Mississippi River; Michigan
2-Michigan; Canada
3-Lake Huron; peninsula
4-Straits of Mackinac; the Buckeye State

1-generally rolling plain with Allegheny Plateau in the East; corn, hay, winter wheat, oats, and soybeans
2-yes; Columbus, OH
3-Marquette (-30°F); Michigan
4-less; Detroit, Saginaw River, Escanaba, Muskegon, Sault Sainte Marie, Port Huron, and Marine City

ANSWERS

Week 16

1-Michigan, Indiana, Illinois, Wisconsin; Lake Superior, Lake Huron, Lake Erie, and Lake Michigan
2-Illinois; Wabash River, Mississippi River, and Lake Michigan
3-Indianapolis; Wabash River
4-cardinal; no

1-Wabash River and Ohio River empty into the Mississippi River; Lake Michigan
2-Lake Michigan, Chicago, IL; East St. Louis, IL
3-southwest; 55,593 square miles, ranked 24th
4-Wisconsin and Michigan; Indianapolis, IN

1-Ft. Wayne; largest area – Allen County / highest population – Marion
2-19%; 4 distinct seasons with a temperate climate
3-40°41'37" N, 89°35'26" W; Iowa
4-it was –27°F, 104 °F; prairie and fertile plains throughout, open hills in the south

Week 17

1-Wisconsin; Mississippi River
2-Lake Superior; yes
3-Lake Superior, Lake Michigan; Mississippi River, St. Croix River
4-MN; Badger State

1-Voyageurs National Park; St. Paul, Minneapolis
2-Michigan, Minnesota, Iowa, and Illinois; Lake Itasca, MN
3-St. Croix River and Mississippi River; north
4-in the northeast corner of Wisconsin on Lake Michigan (answers will vary); Lake Winnebago

1-milk, butter, cheese, and canned and frozen vegetables; lower
2-165 feet, Black River; 44°31'9" N, 88°1'11" W
3-Minnehaha, 53 feet; Minneapolis, MN
4-Big Stone Lake, MN, empties into the Mississippi River; 30%

Week 18

1-eight; Missouri River
2-Iowa; Des Moines River
3-Eastern – Mississippi River, Western – Missouri River; Des Moines
4-Ozarks (Ozark Plateau); St. Louis

1-the northern area is flat, the southern is mountainous; Ozark Plateau
2-toward the Mississippi River; left or east or southeast (any of the three)
3-abundant water for irrigation; Hawkeye State
4-both (this was a tricky one!); Osage River

1-corn; Iowa
2-lower; lower
3-lower; Missouri
4-lower; continental climate, susceptible to cold Canadian air, moist, warm gulf air, and drier southwest air

ANSWERS

Week 19

1-Missouri River; Minnesota
2-Lake Oahe; western
3-South Dakota; Red River
4-Chinese ring-necked pheasant; South Dakota

1-Harney Peak (7243 feet), located in the Black Hills; Lake Traverse and Big Stone Lake
2-wheat; Souris River
3-southwest; White Butte (3506 feet), located in the Badlands or southwest part of the state (answers will vary)
4-in the southwest part of the state; Mount Rushmore

1-710 miles long, originates in Wells County; It was the last major conflict between Indian tribes and U.S. troops where over 200 men, women, and children were killed.
2-elevation 1442 feet, 43°33' N; Big Stone Lake (966 feet)
3-North Dakota: North Dakota
4-yes; extremes of temperature persistent winds, low precipitation and humidity

Week 20

1-Cottonwood; Platte River
2-Mount Rushmore State; Lincoln
3-KS; Kansas River
4-Missouri; Arkansas River

1-Mount Sunflower (4039 feet) located southwest of Goodland, Kansas near the western border; 81,823 square miles, ranked 13nd
2-Sunflower State; trees were scarce
3-farming; North Platte River
4-Colorado; Lewis and Clark Lake

1-Custer County, 3385 square miles difference; Omaha, NE
2-93%*; corn, sorghum, soy beans, hay, wheat, dry beans, oats, potatoes, sugar beets
3-yes; IA, IL, NE, MN, IN, OH, SD, WI, MO, KS, MI, ND (in this order)
4-oak, walnut; 121°F on July 24, 1936

* % of farm land =

$$\frac{\text{farm land area}}{\text{total land area}} \times 100$$

$$\text{square miles} = \frac{\text{acres}}{640}$$

Week 21

1-Saint Paul; northern
2-IA; sunflower
3-western; Madison
4-Montana; NE

1-Mackinac Island; Topeka Kansas
2-Pierre, SD, Bismarck, ND, Jefferson City, MO; west
3-south; Missouri
4-North Star State; Kansas, Minnesota, North Dakota, and Missouri (in that order)

1-Minnesota and Nebraska; -55°F, Feb. 4, 1996
2-tallest building - Sears Tower, Chicago, IL,/tallest structure - TV Tower, Blanchard, ND; 41°4'53" N, 81°31'9" W
3-North Dakota; Kansas, North Dakota
4-Ohio, Illinois, and Michigan; Illinois, Indiana, Iowa, and Minnesota

Please Note:
The secondary level answers could vary from year to year, depending upon what year almanac is used. Most answers were obtained from a 2007 almanac.

ANSWERS

Week 22

1-mostly plains; Red River
2-Gulf of Mexico; Rio Grande River
3-New Mexico; Rocky Mountains
4-Phoenix; eastern

1-SE; AK, TX, NM, AZ, OK
2-Evfavla Lake, Lake Texahoma, and Sardis Lake; the Sooner State
3-Guadalupe Mountains National Park & Big Bend National Park; water
4-Guadalupe Peak (8749 feet), located in the western most part of the state in the national park; TX

1-California; 82°F
2-74103; high plains
3-Texas; shoreline 3359 miles, coastline 367 miles
4-Texas; corn, wheat, and hay

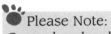 Please Note:
Secondary level answers could vary from year to year, depending upon what year almanac is used. Most answers were obtained from a 2007 almanac.

Week 23

1-Oklahoma City; Lake Texoma
2-Colorado River; TX
3-roadrunner; Santa Fe
4-Colorado River; New Mexico

1-CO, UT, NM, and AZ; Carlsbad Caverns National Park
2-south central; eastern
3-Sonoran Desert; Arizona
4-114,006 square miles, ranked 6th; Humphreys Peak (12,633), located north of Flagstaff, AZ

1-Cherokee, Navajo; record high 128°F on June 29, 1994, record low -40°F on January 7, 1971
2-Grand Canyon in Arizona is 277 miles long, 1 mile deep; 400 miles long, 310 miles wide
3-Red Bluff Reservoir (2842 feet); 1970
4-Texas, Bernalillo

Week 24

1-mountainous; Wyoming
2-no; Great Salt Lake
3-Colorado River; UT
4-Nevada; Lake Tahoe

1-Mount Elbert (14,433 feet) located east of Leadville or west of Colorado Springs, east of Aspen; Mesa Verde National Park
2-west of the continental divide in the central to southwest part of the state (answers will vary); snow skiing
3-in southwestern Wyoming; Pathfinder Reservoir
4-Montana; southeast

1-70%, ranked 31st; sand and gravel, portland cement, crushed stone, gold, and helium
2-higher; 35%
3-Yellowstone, 1872; Wyoming
4-20; mineral extraction, oil, natural gas, tourism, recreation, and agriculture

ANSWERS

Week 25

1-Bighorn River; western
2-Cheyenne; Snake River
3-Lake Pend Oreille (and Priest Lake); Missouri River and Yellowstone River
4-Helena; ponderosa pine

1-Montana and Idaho; Rocky Mountains
2-Treasure State; Granite Peak (12,799 feet), located just northeast of Yellowstone National Park, near the Wyoming border (answers will vary)
3-Wasatch Range; Snake River
4-in central Idaho; 5:30 A.M.

1-Montana; less
2-47°30'N, 111°18'W, 3334 feet elevation; 13*
3-Hells Canyon, 7900 feet deep; about 30%**
4-higher; 11,952 feet

*Montana area divided by 4. (32,760) Compare to area chart of 50 states to find all states with less land area.

**% of U.S. potatoes from Idaho:

$$\frac{\text{Idaho potatoes}}{\text{U.S. potatoes}} \times 100$$

Week 26

1-CO; Salt Lake City
2-Lake Mead; Boise
3-eastern; Wyoming
4-Blue Spruce; South Platte River

1-Beehive State; northwestern region
2-Kings Peak (4123 feet), located in the Unita Mountains, south of the Wyoming border (wording will vary); it is salty
3-109,806, ranked 7th; north and south
4-Great Basin National Park; Lake Tahoe

1-Zion National Park tunnel, 5766 feet; 66.5%
2-Beaver Dam Wash (2000 feet); New Mexico, Colorado, Wyoming, Idaho, Montana
3-gold, sand and gravel, silver, lime, and diatomite; much cleaner
4-gaming, tourism, mining, manufacturing, government, retailing, warehousing, and trucking; 7.5 inches per year, semi arid and arid

Week 27

1-Gila River; mockingbird
2-Black Mesa (4973 feet); Great Plains
3-Colorado, Arizona, New Mexico, and Utah
4-MT; Nevada and Utah

1-Great Salt Lake; Montana
2-Nevada, Arizona, and California; Snake River
3-Yellowstone National Park; Arizona
4-Texas; Oklahoma

1-Franklin Roosevelt; Thomas Foley (D 1989-1995)
2-James Watt, Gail Norton: Oroville Dam, on the Feather River, California
3-Hoover Dam at Lake Mead, NV/AZ border; Anton Anderson Memorial Tunnel in Whittier Alaska, 13,300 feet long
4-Washington; no (Verrazano-Narrows Bridge in New York City is 60 feet longer)

ANSWERS

Week 28

1-Cascade Mountains; Columbia River
2-Olympia; Snake River
3-Pacific Ocean; Salem
4-Canada; OR

1-Mount St. Helens; Strait of Juan de Fuca
2-Olympic National Park; Coast Ranges and Cascade Range
3-NE; Crater Lake
4-NW; 14,410 feet

1-Seattle, WA; western cedar and sitka spruce in Olympic National Park and Coast Douglas fir in the Olympic National Forest
2-farther north; advanced technology, aerospace, biotechnology, international trade, forestry, tourism, recycling, agriculture, and food processing
3-50 feet; Portland, OR
4-greenhouse plants, hay, wheat, grass seed, potatoes, onions, Christmas trees, pears and mint; Douglas fir, hemlock, ponderosa pine

Week 29

1-Sierra Nevada Mountains; Lake Tahoe
2-Califronia redwood; CA
3-Mojave Desert; Oregon
4-Sacramento River; Salton Sea

1-Sierra Nevada Mountains and Coast Ranges; Arizona
2-California; the Golden State
3-8 P.M.; in the southwestern part of California, east of Santa Barbara, CA
4-Golden Gate Bridge, San Francisco Bay; Mount Whitney (14,494 feet), located in Sequoia National Park (answers may vary)

1-Sutro Tower, 1972; 377 miles
2-Death Valley, CA (282 feet below sea level); Yosemite Falls
3-portland cement, sand and gravel, boron, crushed stone, and gold; 48%*
4-agriculture, tourism, apparel, electronics, telecommunications, and entertainment; Sacramento

*% of farm land =

$$\frac{\text{farm land area}}{\text{total land area}} \times 100$$

Week 30

1-volcanoes; Arctic Ocean
2-Yukon River; AK
3-Juneau; Hawaii
4-Hawaii; Honolulu

1-Gates of the Arctic National Park; Barrow, AK
2-Aleutian Islands; southern
3-Bering Strait; Hawaii
4-Kauai and Oahu; Oahu

1-Alaska (answers vary – total area should be close to 571,951 square miles; 31383
2-Texas. Alaska, California; fish products, lumber and pulp, and furs
3-Massachusetts; sugar, pineapples, macadamia nuts, fruits, coffee, vegetables, and floriculture
4-Mount Waialeale, on the island of Kauai, 460 inches per year; 21°18' 25" N 157°51'30" W (or 21° N, 157° W)

Resources

Uncle Josh's Outline Map Book or CD-ROM

These are the outline maps your students will use for their mapping assignments. Includes each U.S. state and much more. Use for both U.S. and World Trail Guides. This is by far one of the best sets of outline maps you'll find. Over 100 maps are available in your choice of reproducible book (112 pages), or CD-ROM usable by all computers that can run Acrobat Reader.

Children's Illustrated Atlas of the United States

This colorful atlas examines each state's unique landscape, culture, and history. It includes maps, photos, symbols, fascinating information, and timelines outlining key events in each state's history. Recommended for answering 5-minute drills and for Points of Interest projects in the *U.S. Trail Guide*. Additional U.S. map features location of Native American tribes. An ideal reference for reports and research projects. 111 pages.

Trail Guide to U.S. Geography Student Notebooks

The Student Notebooks are ready to print from a CD-ROM or downloaded eBook. These are preformatted pages for use with Geography Trails and Points of Interest assignments. Includes generic pages and all outline maps needed. Available for each of the 3 levels in CD-ROM or eBook. Also available with all three levels in one CD-ROM or eBook.

The World Almanac and Book of Facts

Authoritative, comprehensive, and timely information on everything from history, weather, anniversaries, awards, health, nations, presidents, religion, statistics, and so much more - all in one book. Recommended for the Secondary trail in the *Trail Guide to U.S. Geography*, 1008 pages.

The Captain's Dog, My Journey with the Lewis and Clark Tribe

Written by Roland Smith, a delightful narrative on the Lewis and Clark Expedition as seen from the eyes of Lewis's dog, Seaman. Used in the literature unit in the *Trail Guide to U.S. Geography*, 287 pages.

Geography Through Art

A great way to learn about the world and the U.S. is through art. Complete instructions for art projects including sculpture, drawing, pinata, and many more. Organized by continent, all instructions for art projects in the *Trail Guide* series are in this book, 144 pages.

The Ultimate Geography and Timeline Guide

This non-consumable guide is a valuable resource whether you like textbooks, unit studies, notebooking, or classical education. Loaded with activities, flashcards, games, reproducibles, and information for using timelines - all designed to make for a penetrating yet fun study of geography for the whole family, 365 pages.

Trail Guide to World Geography

If you like the format of *Trail Guide to U.S. Geography* then you'll love the world version! Students learn about their world continent by continent with more five-minute daily drills, mapping, building a geography notebook, and choosing from a wide variety of projects, 128 pages.

Trail Guide to Bible Geography

Bible lands version of the Trail Guide series. Makes the Bible come alive as you better understand the geography of this historical region of the world, 128 pages.

Geography Terms Chart

Laminated illustrated color chart with geography terms labeled right on the picture, 16" x 11".

Bibliography

The following resources were used to research state information, questions, and their answers.

Miller, Millie and Nelson, Cyndi. *The United States of America: A State-by-State Guide*. Scholastic, 1999.
Sutcliffe, Andrea. The New York Public Library *Amazing U.S. Geography*. John Wiley and Sons, 2001.
Children's Millennium Atlas of the United States. Rand McNally, 2000.
The World Almanac and Book of Facts 2005. World Almanac Books, 2005.
The World Almanac and Book of Facts 2007. World Almanac Books 2007.
The World Almanac of the U.S.A. World Almanac Books, 1996.